QuickBooks Practice Set

Gain Experience with Realistic Transactions

Michelle L. Long, CPA, MBA

Andrew S. Long, CPA

Copyright © 2015 Michelle L. Long and Andrew S. Long

All rights reserved.

ISBN: 1438298145
ISBN-13: 978-1438298146

DEDICATION

This book is dedicated to all the accountants, bookkeepers and QuickBooks users who want more practice using QuickBooks. We created this practice set for you to gain more experience and confidence using QuickBooks.

ABOUT THE AUTHORS

Michelle L. Long, CPA, MBA is the founder of Long for Success, LLC specializing in QuickBooks consulting and training for accounting professionals and small business owners. She is co-host of the very popular QB Power Hour webinar series (free – http://QBPowerHour.com and the award winning Ultimate Accounting vCon (http://accountingvcon.com).

As an international trainer for Intuit, Michelle has presented hundreds of seminars (and webinars) in cities across the US, Canada, Australia and London, England. In addition, she is a popular speaker at various conferences and has presented webinars for Staples and Office Depot. She has been quoted or mentioned in the New York Times, Inc.com, Business Week, Investor's Business Daily, WebCPA, Accounting Today and more.

Michelle is the author of the books *QuickBooks Practice Set, QuickBooks 2014: On Demand, How to Start a Home-Based Bookkeeping Business* and *Successful QuickBooks Consulting* – all available on Amazon. Plus, she's the author of numerous courses for Intuit Academy and co-author of the Advanced Certifications for QuickBooks Online and QuickBooks desktop.

Michelle is one of the Most Powerful Women in Public Accounting, a Top 10 ProAdvisor (recognized for Social Media), one of 10 Women who Inspire a Profession, a Small Business Influencer, and a Financial Services Champion of the Year by the Small Business Administration in recognition of her dedication to helping entrepreneurs and small business owners.

Michelle is a CPA, Advanced Certified QuickBooks ProAdvisor (both QuickBooks Online and desktop), holds an MBA in Entrepreneurship and is a Certified FastTrac Facilitator. Her blog was named one of *10 Accounting Blogs Worth Watching*. Her Linkedin Group (Successful QuickBooks Online Consultants) has nearly 150,000 members and is a great resource and networking opportunity for accounting professionals.

Andrew S. Long, CPA graduated with a MS in Accountancy from the University of Missouri – Columbia in December 2013. Andrew graduated magna cum laude and he earned numerous scholarships for his academic achievements. Andrew was selected as a member of the prestigious Cornell Leadership Program. He was a member of the Flegel Academy of Aspiring Entrepreneurs and a member of Beta Alpha Psi.

Andrew is a staff accountant for JES Holdings, a residential real estate company in Columbia, Missouri specializing in low-income housing tax credit (LIHTC) properties. He likes water and snow skiing and enjoying the outdoors.

Contents

1 INTRODUCTION 3

2 SET UP A NEW COMPANY 5

    Modify the Chart of Accounts: 7

    Set up Items 8

    Add the following new vendors: 10

    Add the following new customers: 11

    Check your Progress 13

        Home Page 13

        Company Information 14

        Reports 15

        Chart of Accounts 15

        Items list 17

        Vendors List 18

        Customers List 18

3 ENTERING TRANSACTIONS – JANUARY 19

    Notes for entering transactions: 19

    January Transactions 19

    Reconcile Accounts 24

Check Your Progress 27

    Balance Sheet 27

    Profit & Loss 29

    Fixed Asset Items List 30

    Accounts Payable Aging Detail 31

    Open Purchase Orders 32

    Inventory Stock Status by Item 32

    Transaction List by Date 33

4 ENTERING TRANSACTIONS – FEBRUARY 35

Notes for entering transactions: 35

February Transactions 36

Reconcile Accounts 46

Check Your Progress 47

    Balance Sheet 47

    Profit & Loss 49

    Accounts Receivable Aging Detail 50

    Accounts Payable Aging Detail 50

    Sales by Customer Detail 51

    Sales by Item Detail 54

    Inventory Stock Status by Item 58

Transaction List by Date 59

5 ENTERING TRANSACTIONS – MARCH 67

Notes for entering transactions: 67

March Transactions 68

Reconcile Accounts 75

Check Your Results 77

    Balance Sheet 77

    Profit & Loss 79

    Accounts Receivable Aging Detail 80

    Accounts Payable Aging Detail 80

    Open Purchase Orders Detail 81

    Sales by Customer Detail 82

    Sales by Item Detail 86

    Inventory Stock Status by Item 90

    Transaction List by Date 90

ACKNOWLEDGEMENTS

Special thanks to the following individuals for help in reviewing the practice set:

Janice Boggs
JB's Accounting Solutions

Jack E. Cole, Jr.
C*C Systems & Software

Jim Knapp
Knapp Consulting

Jo Ellen Peters
Top Notch Bookkeeping

Paula Small
Small Stepping Stones

Trademarks: Intuit, QuickBooks, QuickBooks Pro, QuickBooks Premier, QuickBooks Accountant, QuickBooks Online, QuickBooks Enterprise, QuickBooks Pro for Mac, ProAdvisor, and all other QuickBooks references are all trademarks or registered trademarks of Intuit, Inc. Microsoft Windows, Word, Excel are all trademarks or registered trademarks of Microsoft; Macintosh (Mac) is a registered trademark of Apple, Inc. All other brands or products are the trademarks or registered trademarks of their respective holders and should be treated as such.

Author: Please direct your comments or suggestions for future editions to michelle@longforsuccess.com or www.LongforSuccess.com.

1 INTRODUCTION

This practice set is designed to provide realistic transactions for a fictional business (Fitness Haven, LLC) to provide experience using QuickBooks. You will set up a new company file, enter three months of transactions, reconcile accounts and check your progress at the end of each month.

This practice set is designed to be used with a windows version of QuickBooks – QuickBooks Pro, Premier, Accountant or Enterprise (but not Simple Start). It could be used with QuickBooks for Mac or QuickBooks Online however not all features or reports may be available in those versions of QuickBooks. We also created a practice set for QuickBooks Online, which was updated in March 2015.

You do not need a specific year of QuickBooks for this practice set. QuickBooks Accountant 2013 was used for the images in this practice set so if you are using another year of QuickBooks, the images may look different. However, entering transactions, reconciling and generating reports are the same in other years of QuickBooks as well.

This practice set does **not** teach you QuickBooks nor accounting or bookkeeping principles. It provides an opportunity for you to get more experience using QuickBooks. The ability to check your progress with various reports helps verify that you are entering transactions correctly.

Additionally, this practice set does **not** address nor discuss accounting principles that may vary according to the type of business entity, industry, etc. To simplify this practice set, Fitness Haven, LLC (the fictitious company used in the practice set) does **not** follow GAAP -- i.e. this exercise does not address unearned revenues on membership dues, depreciation on fixed assets, etc. The focus of this practice set is entering transactions common to most small businesses in QuickBooks, reconciling and generating reports.

Fitness Haven

In this practice set, business partners Tom Martin, Joe Watson, and Nancy Clemens decide to open a neighborhood fitness center called Fitness Haven. They have been discussing the idea for years and finally decided to take the leap and start the business.

The partners will combine money from their savings and take out a bank loan to finance the gym. They have agreed to forgo a salary or compensation for themselves and to not hire any employees until the business is financially stable (i.e. in the practice set there is no payroll, owner's draws or guaranteed payments).

They will manually write checks and use a credit card for purchases. They plan on buying all the equipment and supplies and leasing (renting) the space for Fitness Haven at a popular neighborhood shopping center. The space they are leasing will need remodeling (leasehold improvements) to get it ready to open. They will purchase exercise equipment and offer classes and personal training sessions in addition to monthly or quarterly memberships.

There will be some retail sales from a few inventory items (bottled water, sports drinks, and nutrition bars). They will purchase a cash register and record weekly sales summaries of these retail sales in QuickBooks. All sales are cash or check only (i.e. they do not accept credit cards payments from customers).

You will start by setting up a new company file for Fitness Haven in QuickBooks. Next, you will enter transactions during the start-up phase for the first month (January). Then, there are transactions for the next two months (February and March) as well. There are several reports at the end of each month for you to check your work and make corrections if needed.

NOTE: Your QuickBooks reports will probably look different from the ones in this practice set. To fit the pertinent information from the report onto the page, we customized many reports (i.e. removed columns, changed the width of columns or made other formatting changes). Focus on the content of the reports (the numbers and details) to check your progress.

In QuickBooks, there is no limit to the number of company files. Thus, if you want to start over or go through the practice set again, you can do it. Just go to File > New Company and use a different name than the original name (i.e. Fitness Haven 2 or something different).

Note: Please pay attention to the notes throughout the practice set. They contain helpful information.

2 SET UP A NEW COMPANY

Use the EasyStep Interview to set up the company file. Click Create a New Company and then select Detailed Start. Enter the following information and click next. You can leave other fields blank.

Company name (and Legal Name)	Tax ID	Phone	Address
Fitness Haven, LLC	99-7654321	(654) 555-3476	2601 N Meadow Ln Springfield, IA 68432

Follow the table below to complete the remainder of the setup interview clicking Next to move through the interview.

Prompt	Response
Select your industry	Retail Shop or Online Commerce
How is your company organized?	LLC (Multiple-member - Form 1065)
Select the first month of your fiscal year	January
Set up your administrator password	Choose a password if you wish or leave it blank
Create your company file	Fitness Haven, LLC (click save)
Customizing QuickBooks	
What do you sell?	Both services and products
How will you enter your sales in QuickBooks?	Record each sale individually
Do you charge sales tax?	Yes
Do you want to create estimates in QuickBooks?	No
Tracking customer orders in QuickBooks (applies to QuickBooks Premier, QB Accountant and QB Enterprise Solutions. You will not see it	No

with QB Pro).	
Using statements in QuickBooks	No
Using invoices in QuickBooks	Yes
Using progress invoicing	No
Managing bills you owe	Yes
Tracking inventory in QuickBooks	Yes
Tracking time in QuickBooks	No
Do you have employees?	Yes – Check the box for We have 1099 contractors.
Select a date to start tracking your finances	Beginning of this fiscal year
Review income and expense accounts	Click Next (use default or click Restore Recommendations)

Click Go to Setup to finish the interview and close the setup window.

Modify the Chart of Accounts:

1. Open the Chart of Accounts to edit account names or add new accounts as needed for Tom, Joe, and Nancy so the equity accounts (with sub accounts for Owner's Contributions and Draws) for the partners are as follows:

   - Tom Martin
     - Tom – Owner's Contribution
     - Tom – Owner's Draws
   - Joe Watson
     - Joe – Owner's Contribution
     - Joe – Owner's Draws
   - Nancy Clemens
     - Nancy – Owner's Contribution
     - Nancy – Owner's Draws

2. Add a Credit Card type account named: Visa

3. Add a Long Term Liability account named: Note Payable – Hometown Bank

4. Add Income accounts named Registration Fees and Gym Revenues (for membership fees, classes, and personal training sessions).

Set up Items

Go to the Items List (Items & Services) to add Service items for the monthly classes and personal training sessions. Set up the items to post to the Gym Revenues income account. The classes are $50 each and personal training sessions are $35 an hour. Both are non-taxable.

- Personal Training - $35
- Basic Fitness 101 - $50
- Kardio Killers - $50
- Wicked Weights - $50
- Yoga Fitness - $50

Add the following non-taxable service item to post to the Registration Fees income account:

- Registration Fee ($25)

Add the following non-taxable service items to post to the Gym Revenues income account:

- Monthly memberships ($35)
- Quarterly memberships ($90)

Note: You can delete the consignment item and the non-inventory item – you won't need them.

Fitness Haven will have a few food items (drinks and nutrition bars) available for sale. A cash register will be used to record the sale of food items (inventory). A weekly summary of sales will be recorded in QuickBooks as a Sales Receipt. All sales are paid with cash or checks (no credit cards are accepted from customers).

Add the following inventory items (to be posted to Cost of Goods Sold and Merchandise Sales): The flavor varieties should be set up as sub-items (i.e. Lemon as a sub-item of Sports Drink).

Item	Unit Cost	Sales Price
Bottled Water	$0.17	$1.50
Sports Drink:		
Lemon	0.37	2.00
Orange	0.37	2.00
Blue	0.37	2.00
Red	0.37	2.00
Energy Drink:		
Regular	1.05	3.75
Sugar-Free	1.05	3.75
Nutrition Bar:		
Chocolate	0.45	3.25
Vanilla	0.45	3.25
Peanut Butter	0.45	3.25

Add the following new vendors:

Note: Click on the additional info tab or the tax settings tab to add the 1099 information.

Company	Address	Phone	Eligible for 1099 – ID #
Copper Property Management Co.	423 Eagle Rd Springfield, IA 68432	(654) 555-0122	
Curtis Contractors	8465 Blue Creek Dr Springfield, IA 68432	(654) 555-4876	Yes 99-1234567
Jones Law Firm	493 Bison Ct Springfield, IA 68432	(654) 555-0937	Yes 20-0983456
Life Fitness Co.	12576 Trailview Rd Springfield, IA 68432	(654) 555-4069	

Add the following new customers:

Enter customers with last name, first name for the customer list.

Customer	Address	Phone
Adrian Gonzalez	324 Birdsong Way Springfield, IA 68432	(654) 555-5632
Daniel Brown	782 Locust Ave Springfield, IA 68432	(654) 555-5890
Lucy Hopper	8326 Waterfall Ln Springfield, IA 68432	(654) 555-6264

These are not all the vendors and customers that will be used in this practice set. As you enter transactions for new customers or vendors, use the Quick Add feature to add them.

Note: this practice set contains address information only. In a real business situation, you may need to include more details such as emails, terms, custom fields or more.

Check your Progress

Home Page

This is what the home page looks like based on the preferences entered during the EasyStep Interview.

Note: This is based on using QuickBooks Accountant 2013. Your home page may look slightly different (or include additional icons), but it shouldn't impact your work on the practice set.

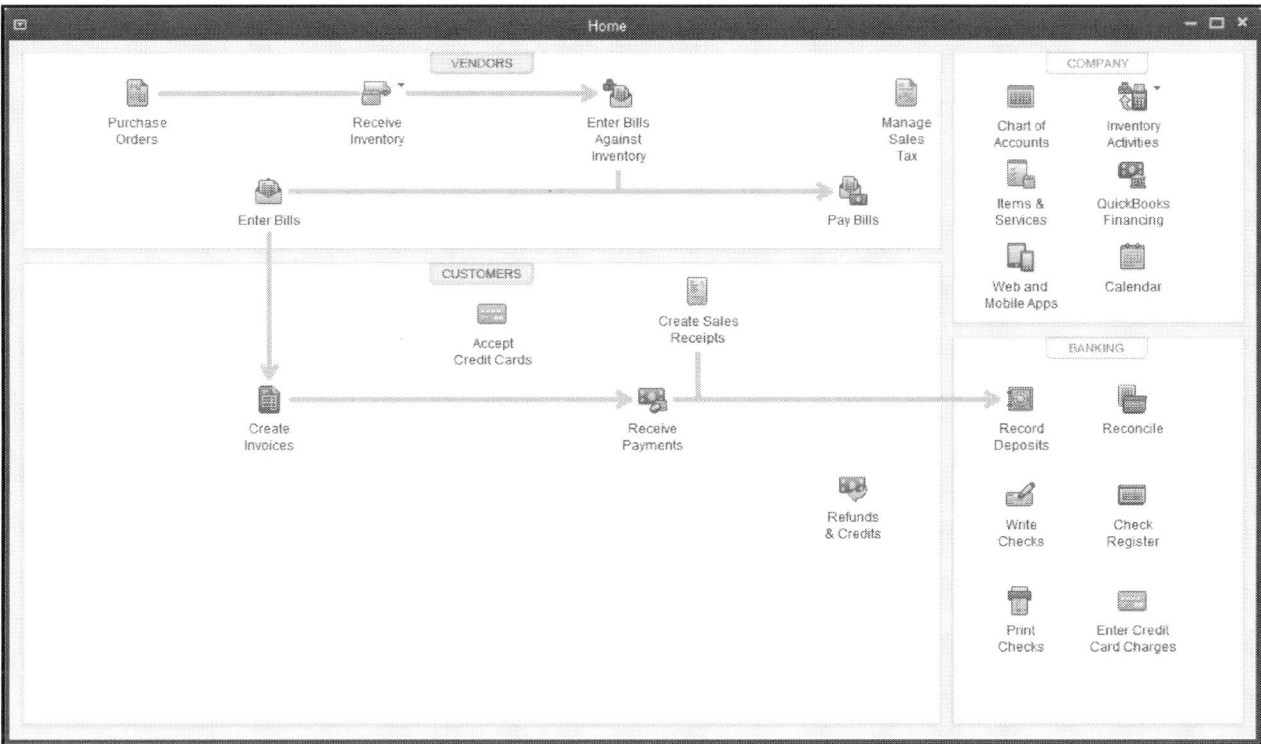

Company Information

Here it what the company information should look like. You can access this by clicking on the company tab and selecting company information. This screen was updated for 2013 and looks different than the older years of QuickBooks. If you're using 2012 or an older year, you should see the company information window which shows the name, address, ID #, etc.

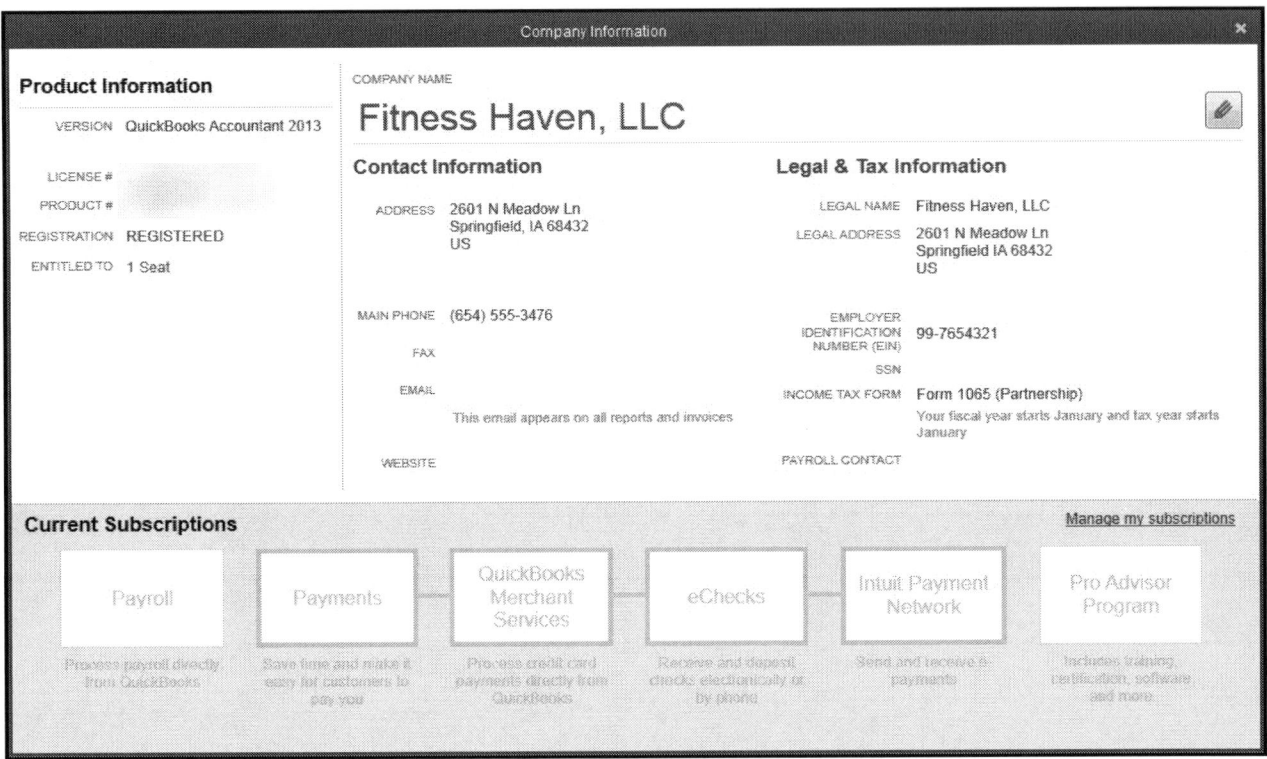

Reports

Chart of Accounts

Here is what the Chart of Accounts looks like. You can access this report by clicking on Reports, List, Account Listing.

Note: For this and all other reports shown throughout the practice set, the reports were modified to show only the most relevant information due to space restrictions so your reports may look different. For example, in this report all columns were removed except the 2 most important columns as shown here.

Account	Type
Inventory Asset	Other Current Asset
Accumulated Depreciation	Fixed Asset
Furniture and Equipment	Fixed Asset
Security Deposits Asset	Other Asset
Visa	Credit Card
Sales Tax Payable	Other Current Liability
Note Payable - Hometown Bank	Long Term Liability
Joe Watson	Equity
Joe Watson:Joe - Owner's Contribution	Equity
Joe Watson:Joe - Owner's Draws	Equity
Nancy Clemens	Equity
Nancy Clemens:Nancy - Owner's Contribution	Equity
Nancy Clemens:Nancy - Owner's Draws	Equity
Opening Balance Equity	Equity
Retained Earnings	Equity
Tom Martin	Equity
Tom Martin:Tom - Owner's Contribution	Equity
Tom Martin:Tom - Owner's Draws	Equity
Gym Revenues	Income
Merchandise Sales	Income
Registration Fees	Income
Sales Discounts	Income
Cost of Goods Sold	Cost of Goods Sold
Merchant Account Fees	Cost of Goods Sold
Advertising and Promotion	Expense
Automobile Expense	Expense
Bank Service Charges	Expense
Computer and Internet Expenses	Expense
Depreciation Expense	Expense

Insurance Expense	Expense
Interest Expense	Expense
Janitorial Expense	Expense
Meals and Entertainment	Expense
Office Supplies	Expense
Professional Fees	Expense
Rent Expense	Expense
Repairs and Maintenance	Expense
Telephone Expense	Expense
Uniforms	Expense
Utilities	Expense
Ask My Accountant	Other Expense

Items list

You can access this report by clicking on Reports, List, Item Listing.

Again – only relevant columns are shown here.

Item	Type	Cost	Price	Sales Tax Code
Basic Fitness 101	Service	0.00	50.00	Non
Kardio Killers	Service	0.00	50.00	Non
Monthly Memberships	Service	0.00	35.00	Non
Personal Training	Service	0.00	35.00	Non
Quarterly Memberships	Service	0.00	90.00	Non
Registration Fee	Service	0.00	25.00	Non
Wicked Weights	Service	0.00	50.00	Non
Yoga Fitness	Service	0.00	50.00	Non
Bottled Water	Inventory Part	0.17	1.50	Tax
Energy Drink	Inventory Part	0.00	0.00	Tax
Energy Drink:Regular	Inventory Part	1.05	3.75	Tax
Energy Drink:Sugar-Free	Inventory Part	1.05	3.75	Tax
Nutrition Bar	Inventory Part	0.00	0.00	Tax
Nutrition Bar:Chocolate	Inventory Part	0.45	3.25	Tax
Nutrition Bar:Peanut Butter	Inventory Part	0.45	3.25	Tax
Nutrition Bar:Vanilla	Inventory Part	0.45	3.25	Tax
Sports Drink	Inventory Part	0.00	0.00	Tax
Sports Drink:Blue	Inventory Part	0.37	2.00	Tax
Sports Drink:Lemon	Inventory Part	0.37	2.00	Tax
Sports Drink:Orange	Inventory Part	0.37	2.00	Tax
Sports Drink:Red	Inventory Part	0.37	2.00	Tax
Non-inventory Item	Non-inventory Part	0.00	0.00	Tax
Local Tax	Sales Tax Item	0.00	0.0%	
Out of State	Sales Tax Item	0.00	0.0%	
State Tax	Sales Tax Item	0.00	0.0%	

Vendors List

You can view the vendors list by clicking on Reports, List, Vendor Contact List.

Vendor	Bill from	Main Phone
Copper Property Management Co.	423 Eagle Rd Springfield, IA 68432	(654) 555-0122
Curtis Contractors	8465 Blue Creek Dr Springfield, IA 68432	(654) 555-4876
Jones Law Firm	493 Bison Ct Springfield, IA 68432	(654) 555-0937
Life Fitness Co.	12576 Trailview Rd Springfield, IA 68432	(654) 555-4069

Customers List

You can view the customers list by clicking on Reports, List, Customer Contact List.

Customer	Bill to	Main Phone
Brown, Daniel	782 Locust Ave Springfield, IA 68432	(654) 555-5890
Gonzalez, Adrian	324 Birdsong Way Springfield, IA 68432	(654) 555-5632
Hopper, Lucy	8326 Waterfall Ln Springfield, IA 68432	(654) 555-6264

3 ENTERING TRANSACTIONS – JANUARY

Enter the following transactions for January. For this practice set, post the following transactions to the appropriate account based on the expenditure (i.e. do not post anything to start-up expenses). In a real situation, you may need to consult with an accountant or tax professional for guidance on accounting for start-up costs.

Notes for entering transactions:

- Use Accounts Payable for monthly expenses and bills. When transactions say "Received a Bill" (Enter a Bill) and Pay Bills when indicated.

- Enter Checks or Credit Card Charges as indicated for purchases from local retailers and others.

- Quick Add Customers and Vendors as needed.

- Create new accounts as needed.

January Transactions

1. Jan 4: The partners (Tom Martin, Joe Watson, and Nancy Clemens) contribute $5,000.00 each to open the Fitness Haven checking account at Hometown Bank with an initial deposit totaling $15,000.00.

    Note: Add a bank account for Hometown Bank. Enter a deposit for the $15,000 posting it to the Owner's Contribution accounts for each partner. Quick Add each partner as a Vendor so details of their activity will be shown in the Vendor Center.

    Note: You may want to go to Edit, Preferences, Accounting, Company Preferences and uncheck so it will not warn you about transactions entered more than 90 days in the past. Additionally, you may want to go to the General Preferences, My Preferences and check to have it use the last date entered (vs. Today's date). You can use the + or – key to move the date forward or backward quickly as you enter transactions.

2. Jan 7: Deposited loan proceeds of $250,000.00 for the Note Payable from Hometown Bank into checking account.

    Note: Do not use loan manger.

3. Jan 8: Check #1001 to Copper Property Management Co. in the amount of $4,500.00 ($3,000.00 for security deposit and $1,500.00 for January rent).

   Note: Make sure to uncheck print later in order to enter the check number.

4. Jan 9: Check #1002 to Jones Law Firm in the amount of $1,785.00 for legal fees for the partnership agreement.

   Note: Create a new expense account for Legal Fees as a sub account of Professional Fees.

5. Jan 17: Check #1003 to Curtis Contractors in the amount of $52,736.89 for leasehold improvements (create a new fixed asset account).

   Note: This practice set will not calculate and record depreciation expense.

6. Jan 18: Check #1004 to Life Fitness Co. in the amount of $80,000.00 for the purchase of exercise equipment.

Fixed Asset Item	Total Price
Treadmills (5)	$10,000
Stationary Bikes (5)	12,000
Elliptical Machines (5)	10,000
Weight Machines (10)	40,000
Free Weights (2 sets)	8,000

Note: Add the equipment purchased to the Fixed Asset Item List (via the Items tab on the check) and post it to the Furniture and Equipment account. To save time, you can add one item for Treadmills and note in the description that it was for 5 Treadmills.

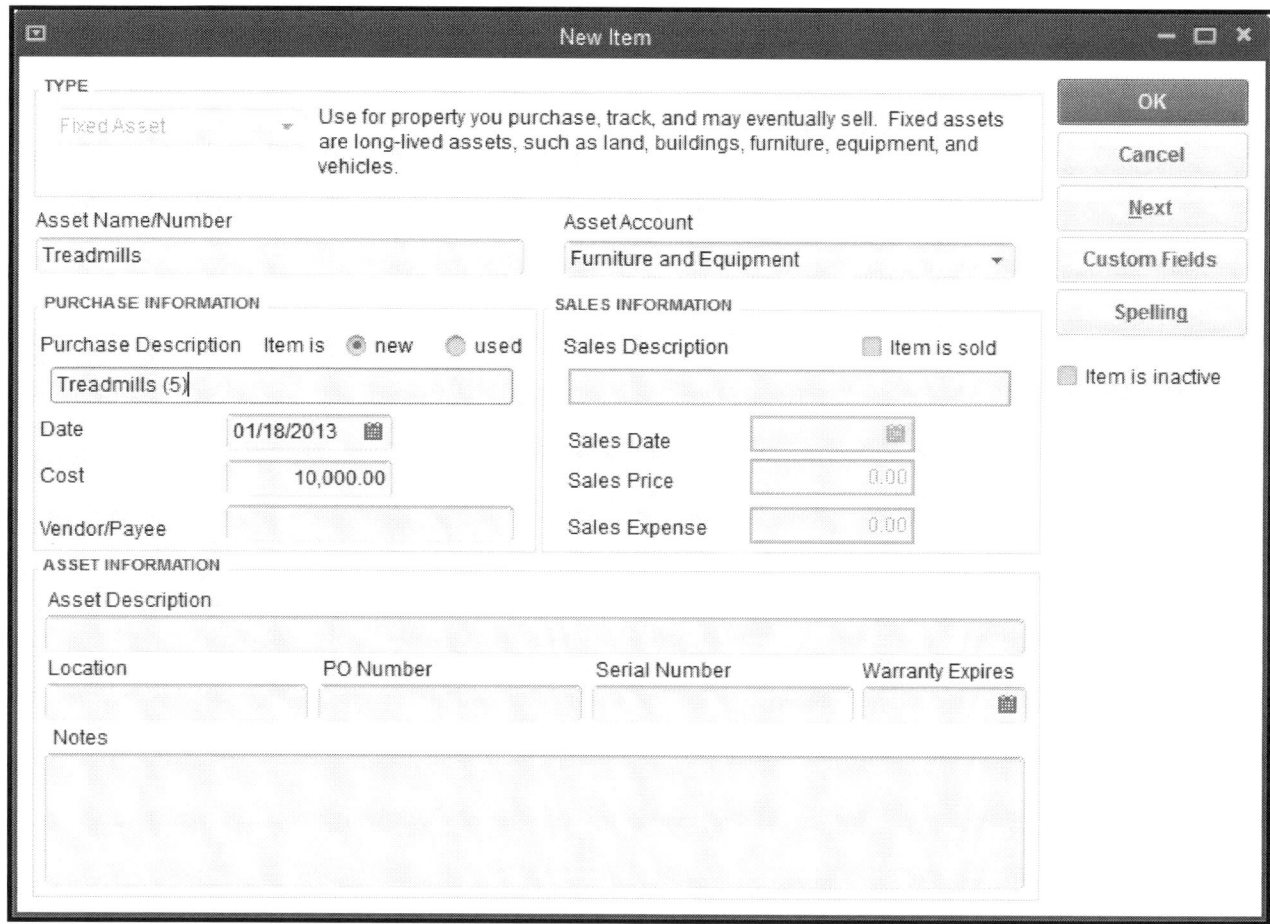

7. Jan 21: Charged $136.67 on Visa credit card at Wal-Mart for office supplies.

8. Jan 21: Check #1005 to Costco in the amount of $2,400 for the following office equipment:

   Note: Add the equipment purchased to the Fixed Asset Item List and post it to a new account called Office Furniture and Equipment.

Fixed Asset Item	Total Price
Cash Register	$1,200
Computer	1,000
Printer	200

9. Jan 22: Purchase order #1 to Fit Foods, Inc. in the amount of $126.48 to purchase the following inventory items:

Item	Quantity	Unit Cost	Total Cost	Sales Price
Bottled Water	48	$0.17	$8.16	$1.50
Sports Drink:				
Lemon	24	0.37	8.88	2.00
Orange	24	0.37	8.88	2.00
Blue	24	0.37	8.88	2.00
Red	24	0.37	8.88	2.00
Energy Drink:				
Regular	24	1.05	25.20	3.75
Sugar-Free	24	1.05	25.20	3.75
Nutrition Bar:				
Chocolate	24	0.45	10.80	3.25
Vanilla	24	0.45	10.80	3.25
Peanut Butter	24	0.45	10.80	3.25

10. Jan 23: Check #1006 to Geek Squad for computer and internet expenses in the amount of $250.00 to set up and configure computers and network.

11. Jan 25: Check #1007 to Super Signs in the amount of $1,200.00 for purchase of outdoor signage (fixed asset, furniture and equipment account).

12. Jan 26: Check #1008 to ABC Web Designs in the amount of $300.00 for website creation (a computer and internet expense).

13. Jan 28: Check #1009 to Val-Pak in the amount of $225.00 for advertising in their direct mail packet.

14. Jan 29: Charged $1,723.15 on Visa credit card at Office Depot for the following office furniture:

Fixed Asset Item	Total Price
Desk (2)	$1,567.39
Chairs (2)	155.76

15. Jan 31: Received bill from Time Warner in the amount of $147.62 for phone and internet service with terms of net 30 (n/30).

    Note: Make Phone/Internet a subaccount of utilities expense. Also create a subaccount for the following three bills (electricity, water, trash removal).

16. Jan 31: Received bill from Metro Electric Co. in the amount of $183.86 for electricity with terms of n/30.

17. Jan 31: Received bill from City of Springfield in the amount of for $51.45 for water with terms of n/30.

18. Jan 31: Received bill from Waste Management in the amount of $45.00 for trash removal with terms of n/30.

Reconcile Accounts

Use the following information to reconcile the checking account:

Bank Statement Ending Date	1/31/2015
Bank Statement Ending Balance	$122,128.11
Outstanding Checks: Check #1008 -- $300 Check #1009 -- $225	

```
10:43 PM                        Fitness Haven, LLC
01/16/13                       Reconciliation Detail
                        Fitness Haven, Period Ending 01/31/2013

         Type          Date       Num     Name              Clr    Amount        Balance
     Beginning Balance                                                            0.00
         Cleared Transactions
             Checks and Payments - 7 items
     Check            01/08/2013   1001    Copper Property M...  X   -4,500.00    -4,500.00
     Check            01/09/2013   1002    Jones Law Firm        X   -1,785.00    -6,285.00
     Check            01/17/2013   1003    Curtis Contractors    X  -52,736.89   -59,021.89
     Check            01/18/2013   1004    Life Fitness Co.      X  -80,000.00  -139,021.89
     Check            01/21/2013   1005    Costco                X   -2,400.00  -141,421.89
     Check            01/23/2013   1006    Geek Squad            X     -250.00  -141,671.89
     Check            01/25/2013   1007    Super Sings           X   -1,200.00  -142,871.89
             Total Checks and Payments                             -142,871.89  -142,871.89

             Deposits and Credits - 2 items
     Deposit          01/04/2013                                X   15,000.00    15,000.00
     Deposit          01/07/2013                                X  250,000.00   265,000.00
             Total Deposits and Credits                              265,000.00   265,000.00

         Total Cleared Transactions                                  122,128.11   122,128.11

     Cleared Balance                                                 122,128.11   122,128.11

         Uncleared Transactions
             Checks and Payments - 2 items
     Check            01/26/2013   1008    ABC Web Designs            -300.00      -300.00
     Check            01/28/2013   1009    Val-Pak                    -225.00      -525.00
             Total Checks and Payments                                  -525.00      -525.00

         Total Uncleared Transactions                                   -525.00      -525.00

     Register Balance as of 01/31/2013                                121,603.11   121,603.11

     Ending Balance                                                   121,603.11   121,603.11
```

Use the following information to reconcile the Visa credit card account:

Bank Statement Ending Date	1/31/2015
Bank Statement Ending Balance	$1,859.82
Outstanding Items: None	

After reconciling the credit card account, select to write a check for payment now. Enter the payment date of Feb. 1, payable to Great American Bank (Quick Add as a vendor). The check number is 1010.

```
10:48 PM                          Fitness Haven, LLC
01/16/13                         Reconciliation Detail
                              Visa, Period Ending 01/31/2013

        Type            Date       Num        Name         Clr      Amount        Balance
  Beginning Balance                                                                  0.00
      Cleared Transactions
          Charges and Cash Advances - 2 items
  Credit Card Charge  01/21/2013           Wal-Mart         X       -136.67        -136.67
  Credit Card Charge  01/29/2013           Office Depot     X     -1,723.15      -1,859.82
              Total Charges and Cash Advances                     -1,859.82      -1,859.82

          Total Cleared Transactions                              -1,859.82      -1,859.82

  Cleared Balance                                                  1,859.82       1,859.82

  Register Balance as of 01/31/2013                                1,859.82       1,859.82

  Ending Balance                                                   1,859.82       1,859.82
```

QUICKBOOKS PRACTICE SET

Check Your Progress

Create the following reports and compare them to the results shown. Make sure you change the report date for this and all other reports so that it displays the proper period (in this case as of 1/31/13). Throughout this practice set, you may notice the reports shown look different than the reports you generate (some columns missing, different column widths, etc.). This is due space constraints which require customizing the reports to fit in this practice set. These differences are cosmetic only; the numbers shown should match your own.

Balance Sheet

Note: This report can be found by clicking on Reports, Company & Financial, Balance Sheet Standard.

	Jan 31, 13
ASSETS	
Current Assets	
Checking/Savings	
Hometown Bank - Checking	121,603.11
Total Checking/Savings	121,603.11
Total Current Assets	121,603.11
Fixed Assets	
Furniture and Equipment	81,200.00
Leasehold Improvements	52,736.89
Office Furniture and Equipment	4,123.15
Total Fixed Assets	138,060.04
Other Assets	
Security Deposits Asset	3,000.00
Total Other Assets	3,000.00
TOTAL ASSETS	262,663.15
LIABILITIES & EQUITY	
Liabilities	
Current Liabilities	
Accounts Payable	
Accounts Payable	427.93
Total Accounts Payable	427.93

Credit Cards	
Visa	1,859.82
Total Credit Cards	1,859.82
Total Current Liabilities	2,287.75
Long Term Liabilities	
Note Payable - Hometown Bank	250,000.00
Total Long Term Liabilities	250,000.00
Total Liabilities	252,287.75
Equity	
Joe Watson	
Joe - Owner's Contribution	5,000.00
Total Joe Watson	5,000.00
Nancy Clemens	
Nancy - Owner's Contribution	5,000.00
Total Nancy Clemens	5,000.00
Tom Martin	
Tom - Owner's Contribution	5,000.00
Total Tom Martin	5,000.00
Net Income	-4,624.60
Total Equity	10,375.40
TOTAL LIABILITIES & EQUITY	262,663.15

Profit & Loss

Note: This report can be found by clicking on Reports, Company & Financial, Profit & Loss Standard.

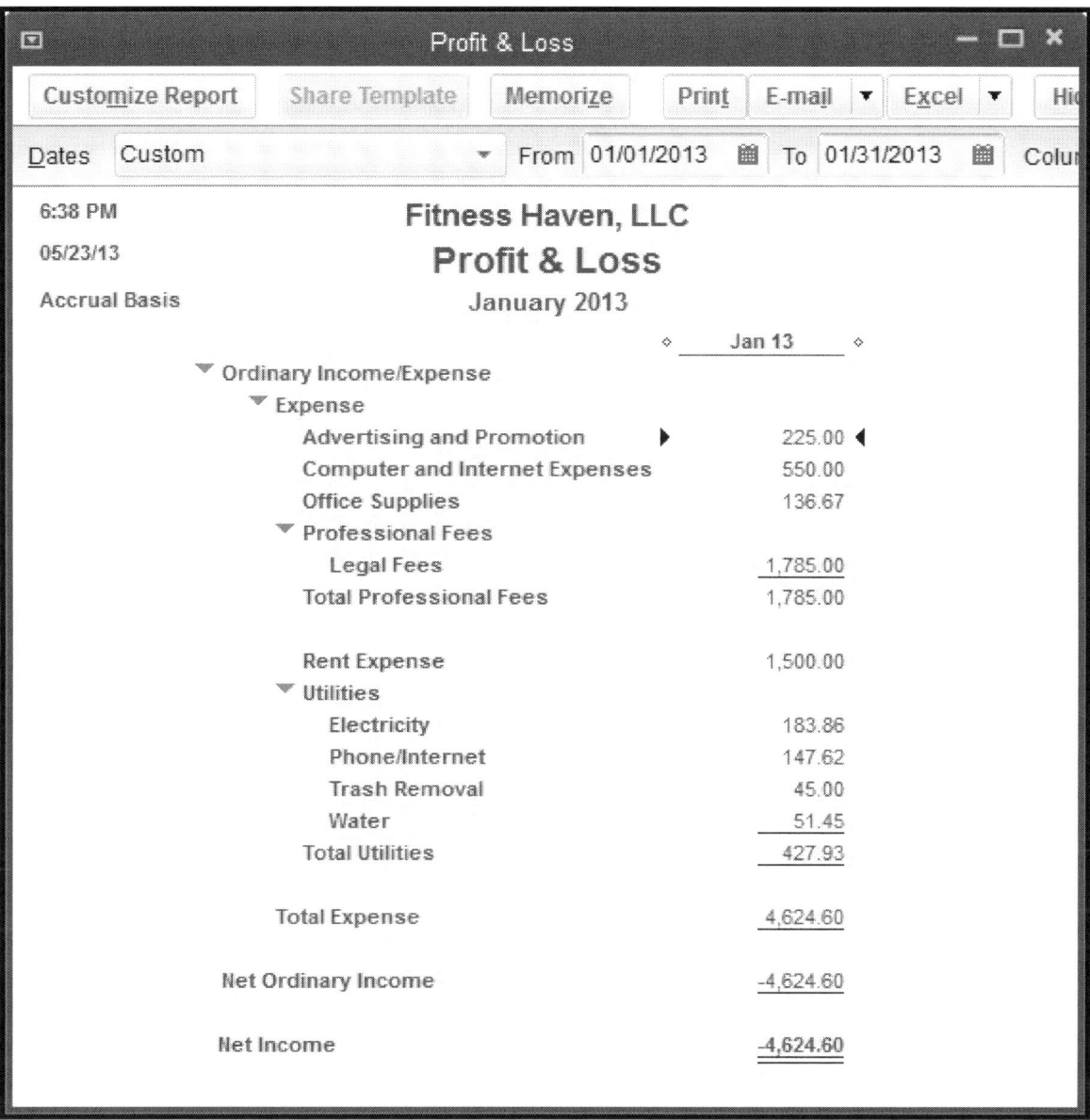

Fixed Asset Items List

Note: This report can be found by clicking on Reports, List, Fixed Asset Listing.

Accounts Payable Aging Detail

Note: This report can be found by clicking on Reports, Vendors and Payables, A/P Aging Detail.

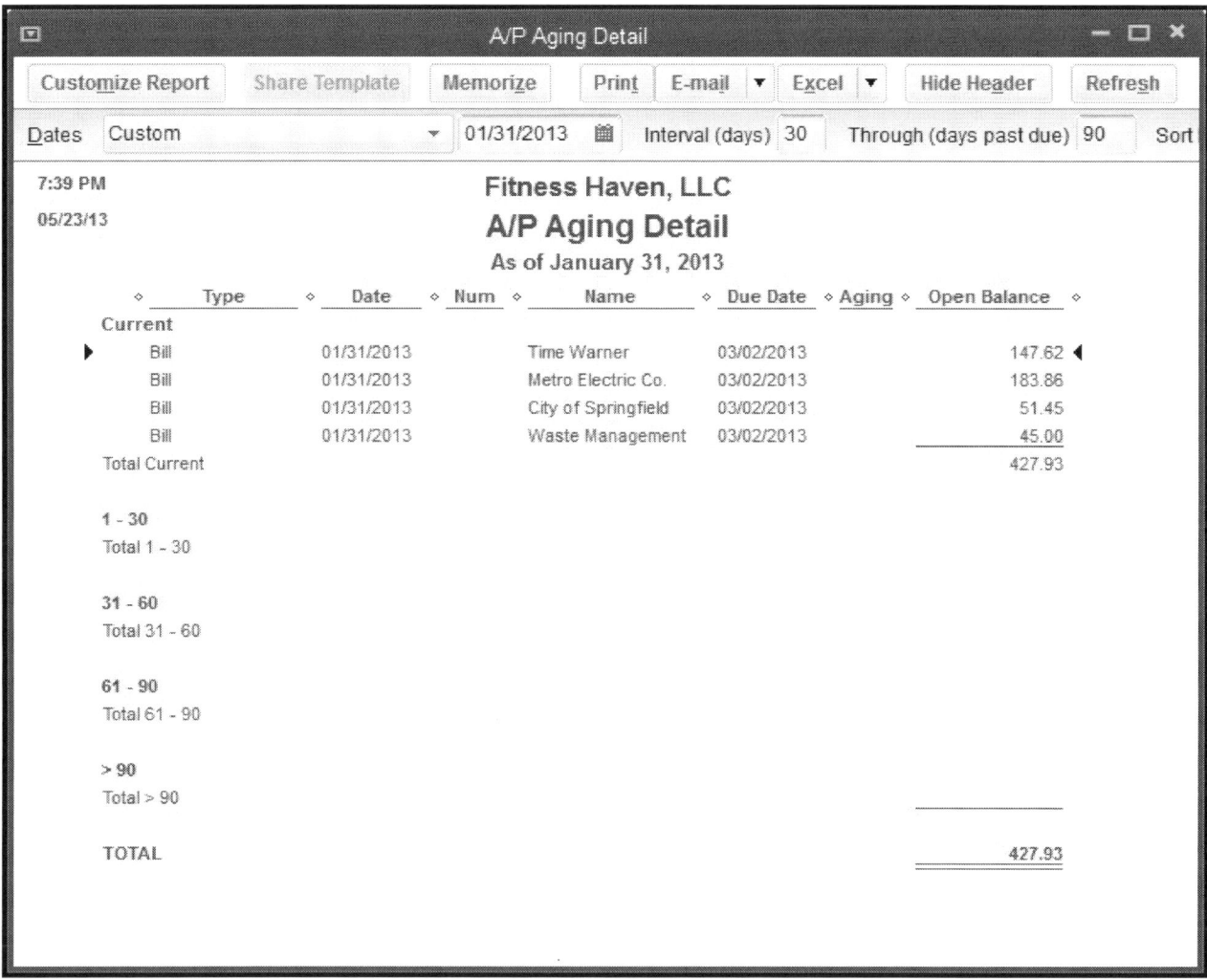

Open Purchase Orders

Note: This report can be found by clicking on Reports, Purchases, Open Purchase Orders. It is ok if you see a different delivery date – don't worry about it. It won't affect anything—just ignore it.

Type	Date	Name	Num	Deliv Date	Amount	Open Balance
Purchase Order	01/22/2015	Fit Foods, Inc.	1	01/21/2015	126.48	126.48
Total					**126.48**	**126.48**

Inventory Stock Status by Item

Note: This report can be found by clicking on Reports, Inventory, Inventory Stock Status by Item.

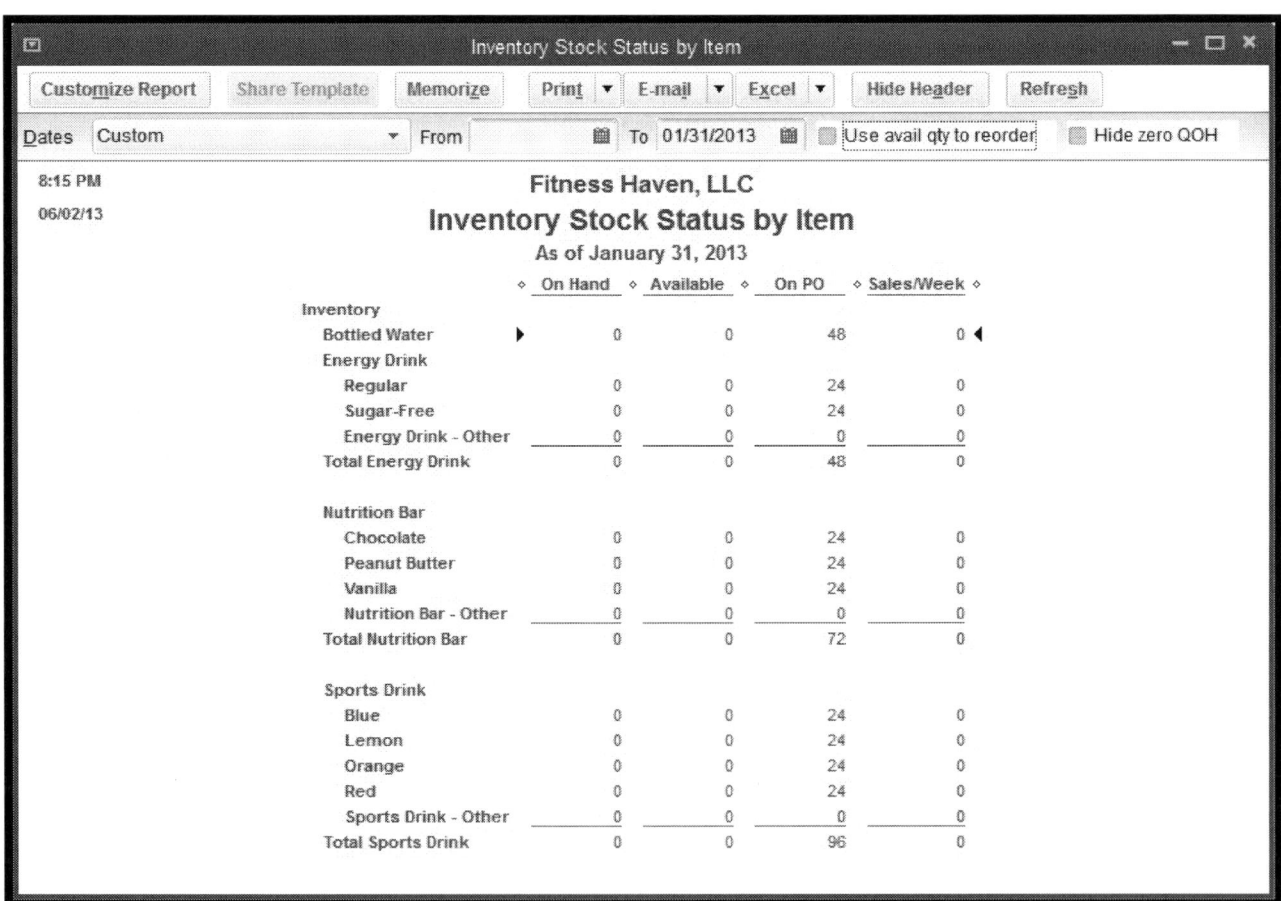

QUICKBOOKS PRACTICE SET

Transaction List by Date

Note: This report can be found by clicking on Reports, Accountant & Taxes, Transaction List by Date. Then, to get the details click on Customize, Filter, Summary Only and Remove Filter.

Type	Date	Num	Name	Account	Split	Debit	Credit
Deposit	01/04/2015			Hometown Bank	-SPLIT-	15,000.00	
Deposit	01/04/2015		Tom Martin	Tom - Owner's Contribution	Hometown Bank		5,000.00
Deposit	01/04/2015		Joe Watson	Joe - Owner's Contribution	Hometown Bank		5,000.00
Deposit	01/04/2015		Nancy Clemens	Nancy - Owner's Contribution	Hometown Bank		5,000.00
Deposit	01/07/2015			Hometown Bank	Note Payable - Hometown Bank	250,000.00	
Deposit	01/07/2015		Hometown Bank	Note Payable - Hometown Bank	Hometown Bank		250,000.00
Check	01/08/2015	1001	Copper Property Management Co	Hometown Bank	-SPLIT-		4,500.00
Check	01/08/2015	1001	Copper Property Management Co	Security Deposits Asset	Hometown Bank	3,000.00	
Check	01/08/2015	1001	Copper Property Management Co	Rent Expense	Hometown Bank	1,500.00	
Check	01/09/2015	1002	Jones Law Firm	Hometown Bank	Legal Fees		1,785.00
Check	01/09/2015	1002	Jones Law Firm	Legal Fees	Hometown Bank	1,785.00	
Check	01/17/2015	1003	Curtis Contractors	Hometown Bank	Leasehold Improvements		52,736.89
Check	01/17/2015	1003	Curtis Contractors	Leasehold Improvements	Hometown Bank	52,736.89	
Check	01/18/2015	1004	Life Fitness Co.	Hometown Bank	-SPLIT-		80,000.00
Check	01/18/2015	1004	Life Fitness Co.	Furniture and Equipment	Hometown Bank	10,000.00	
Check	01/18/2015	1004	Life Fitness Co.	Furniture and Equipment	Hometown Bank	12,000.00	
Check	01/18/2015	1004	Life Fitness Co.	Furniture and Equipment	Hometown Bank	10,000.00	
Check	01/18/2015	1004	Life Fitness Co.	Furniture and Equipment	Hometown Bank	40,000.00	
Check	01/18/2015	1004	Life Fitness Co.	Furniture and Equipment	Hometown Bank	8,000.00	
Credit Card Charge	01/21/2015		Wal-Mart	Visa	Office Supplies		136.67
Credit Card Charge	01/21/2015		Wal-Mart	Office Supplies	Visa	136.67	
Check	01/21/2015	1005	Costco	Hometown Bank	-SPLIT-		2,400.00
Check	01/21/2015	1005	Costco	Office Furniture & Equipment	Hometown Bank	1,200.00	
Check	01/21/2015	1005	Costco	Office Furniture & Equipment	Hometown Bank	1,000.00	
Check	01/21/2015	1005	Costco	Office Furniture & Equipment	Hometown Bank	200.00	
Check	01/23/2015	1006	Geek Squad	Hometown Bank	Computer and Internet Expenses		250.00
Check	01/23/2015	1006	Geek Squad	Computer and Internet Expenses	Hometown Bank	250.00	
Check	01/25/2015	1007	Super Signs	Hometown Bank	Furniture and Equipment		1,200.00
Check	01/25/2015	1007	Super Signs	Furniture and Equipment	Hometown Bank	1,200.00	
Check	01/26/2015	1008	ABC Web Designs	Hometown Bank	Computer and Internet Expenses		300.00
Check	01/26/2015	1008	ABC Web Designs	Computer and Internet Expenses	Hometown Bank	300.00	

Type	Date	Num	Name	Account	Split	Amount
Check	01/28/2015	1009	Val-Pak	Hometown Bank	Advertising and Promotion	225.00
Check	01/28/2015	1009	Val-Pak	Advertising and Promotion	Hometown Bank	225.00
Credit Card Charge	01/29/2015		Office Depot	Visa	-SPLIT-	1,723.15
Credit Card Charge	01/29/2015		Office Depot	Office Furniture & Equipment	Visa	1,567.39
Credit Card Charge	01/29/2015		Office Depot	Office Furniture & Equipment	Visa	155.76
Bill	01/31/2015		Time Warner	Accounts Payable	Phone / Internet	147.62
Bill	01/31/2015		Time Warner	Phone / Internet	Accounts Payable	147.62
Bill	01/31/2015		Metro Electric	Accounts Payable	Electricity	183.86
Bill	01/31/2015		Metro Electric	Electricity	Accounts Payable	183.86
Bill	01/31/2015		City of Springfield	Accounts Payable	Water	51.45
Bill	01/31/2015		City of Springfield	Water	Accounts Payable	51.45
Bill	01/31/2015		Waste Management	Accounts Payable	Trash Removal	45.00
Bill	01/31/2015		Waste Management	Trash Removal	Accounts Payable	45.00

4 ENTERING TRANSACTIONS – FEBRUARY

Fitness Haven opens on February 4th and offers two membership options.
- **Monthly**: New members pay a one-time registration fee of $25 and $35 month membership fees.
- **Quarterly**: Members pay three months of membership dues in advance (only $30 / month). The 3 month membership is non-refundable.

Notes for entering transactions:

- Use a Sales Receipt for initial registration fees and membership dues received. Subsequent membership dues will be entered as an Invoice and then Receive Payment.
- Enter Sales Receipts for classes and personal training sessions.
- The default in QuickBooks should be for payments received to go to Undeposited Funds. Leave payments in Undeposited Funds until the transaction (weekly) to Record Deposits.
- Use Accounts Payable (i.e. Enter Bills and Pay Bills) for monthly expenses and bills (when transactions say Received Bill and Pay Bills).
- Enter Checks as indicated for purchases from local retailers and others.
- Do not worry about depreciation on fixed assets. It is assumed the accountant or tax professional maintains details of fixed assets and depreciation.

February Transactions

1. Feb 1: Check #1011 to Oak Hill Homeowners Association in the amount of $150.00 for an ad in their newsletter.

2. Feb 3: Check #1012 to Willy's Windows in the amount of $75.00 for window cleaning (repairs and maintenance).

3. Feb 3: Received inventory and the bill ($126.48) from Fit Foods, Inc. for all items ordered on Purchase Order #1, the terms are n/30.

4. Feb 4: Lucy Steele paid $25 for a first time gym registration fee and a monthly membership fee of $35 (total received $60). (Enter a Sales Receipt)

5. Feb 4: Jerry Kline paid $25 for a first time gym registration fee and a monthly membership fee of $35 (total received $60). (Sales Receipt)

6. Feb 4: Received bill from Yoga Bliss, LLC in the amount of $235.00 for yoga mats and towels (i.e. fitness supplies – create a new expense account) with terms of 2% 10, Net 30.

7. Feb 4: Jim Hill paid $25 for a first time gym registration fee and a monthly membership fee of $35. (Sales Receipt)

8. Feb 4: Augusto Gutierrez paid $90 for a Quarterly Membership (i.e. 3 months of gym membership). For Quarterly memberships, the monthly rate is discounted to $30/month and the registration fee is waived because of prepayment. (Sales Receipt)

9. Feb 5: Check #1013 to Long for Success, LLC in the amount of $450.00 for QuickBooks setup and training (Create a new account for accounting fees as a sub account of Professional Fees).

10. Feb 6: Sent invoices to Adrian Gonzalez, Daniel Brown, Lucy Hopper in the amount of $35 each for February gym membership (Monthly membership) with terms of n/10. (Their gym registration fee was waived because they signed up in advance). Edit the customer to set up the terms of net 10). If you have QuickBooks 2012 or newer, you can create Batch Invoices (under the Customer menu). Otherwise, enter each invoice separately.

11. Feb 7: The following table lists the members who signed up and paid for February fitness classes (i.e. enter a Sales Receipt for each one). All classes are $50.

Basic Fitness 101	Wicked Weights	Kardio Killers	Yoga Fitness
Jerry Kline	Daniel Brown		
Adrian Gonzalez	Jim Hill		
Lucy Steele			

12. Feb 7: Tim Barnes paid $25 for a first time gym registration fee and a monthly membership fee of $35. (Sales Receipt)

13. Feb 7: Sold 1 hour of personal training to Tim Barnes for $35. (Sales Receipt)

14. Feb 7: Received payment of $35 from Adrian Gonzalez for February gym membership.

15. Feb 7: Total food sales from the week are shown in the table on the next page:

Note: Add a new Sales Tax Item for Springfield, 8% payable to Iowa Department of Revenue. Then, add a customer named Weekly Sales as taxable with the Springfield tax rate. Then enter a Sales Receipt for the weekly sales.

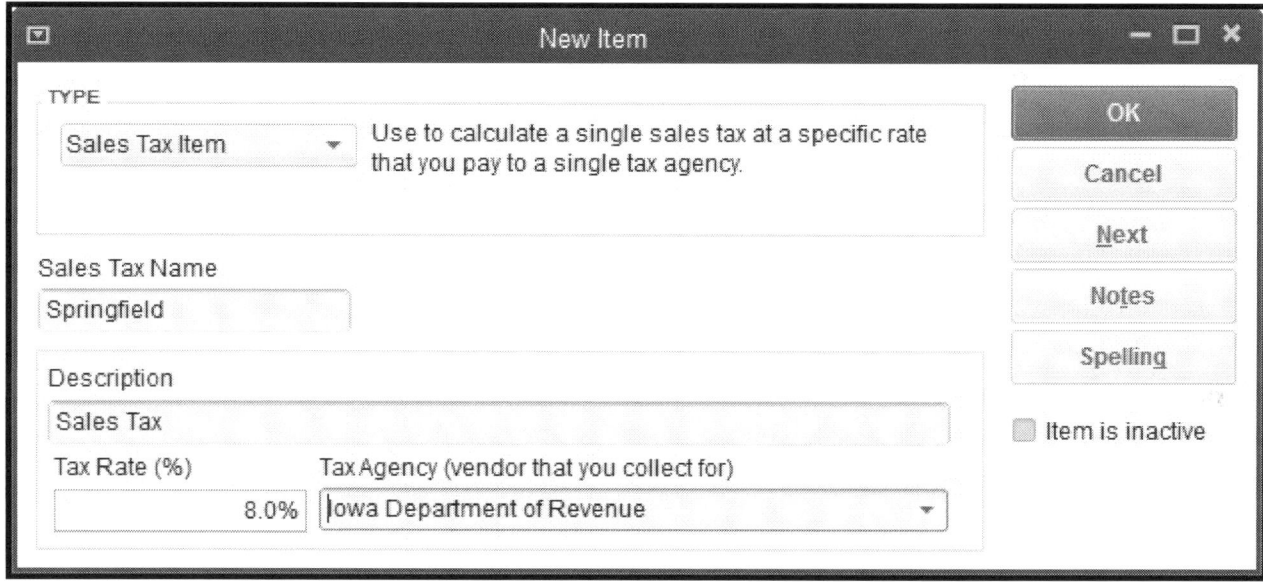

Item	Quantity Sold	Sales Price	Totals
Bottled Water		$1.50	
Sports Drink:			
Lemon		2.00	
Orange	2	2.00	$4.00
Blue	2	2.00	4.00
Red		2.00	
Energy Drink:			
Regular		3.75	
Sugar-Free		3.75	
Nutrition Bar:			
Chocolate	1	3.25	3.25
Vanilla		3.25	
Peanut Butter		3.25	
Subtotal			**11.25**
Sales Tax			**0.90**
Total			**12.15**

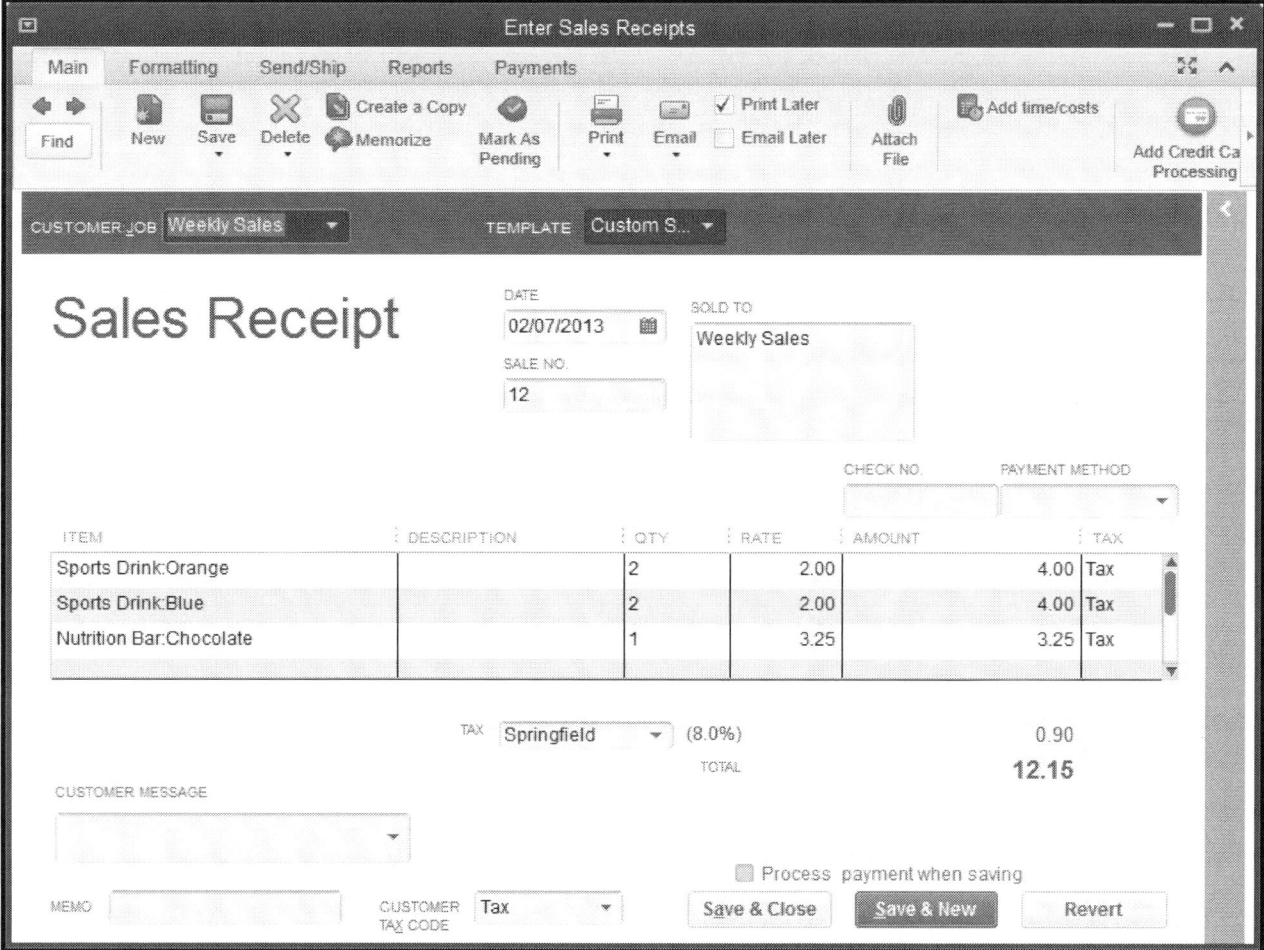

16. Feb 7: Deposited all Undeposited funds from the first week of the month into the checking account (total deposit $662.15).

17. Feb 8: Recorded inventory adjustment: loss of 6 sugar-free energy drinks. A 6-pack of drinks was dropped and all cans were punctured.

   Note: Set up an expense account called Damaged Inventory to record the adjustment. (Click on Inventory Activities, Adjust Quantity/Value on Hand).

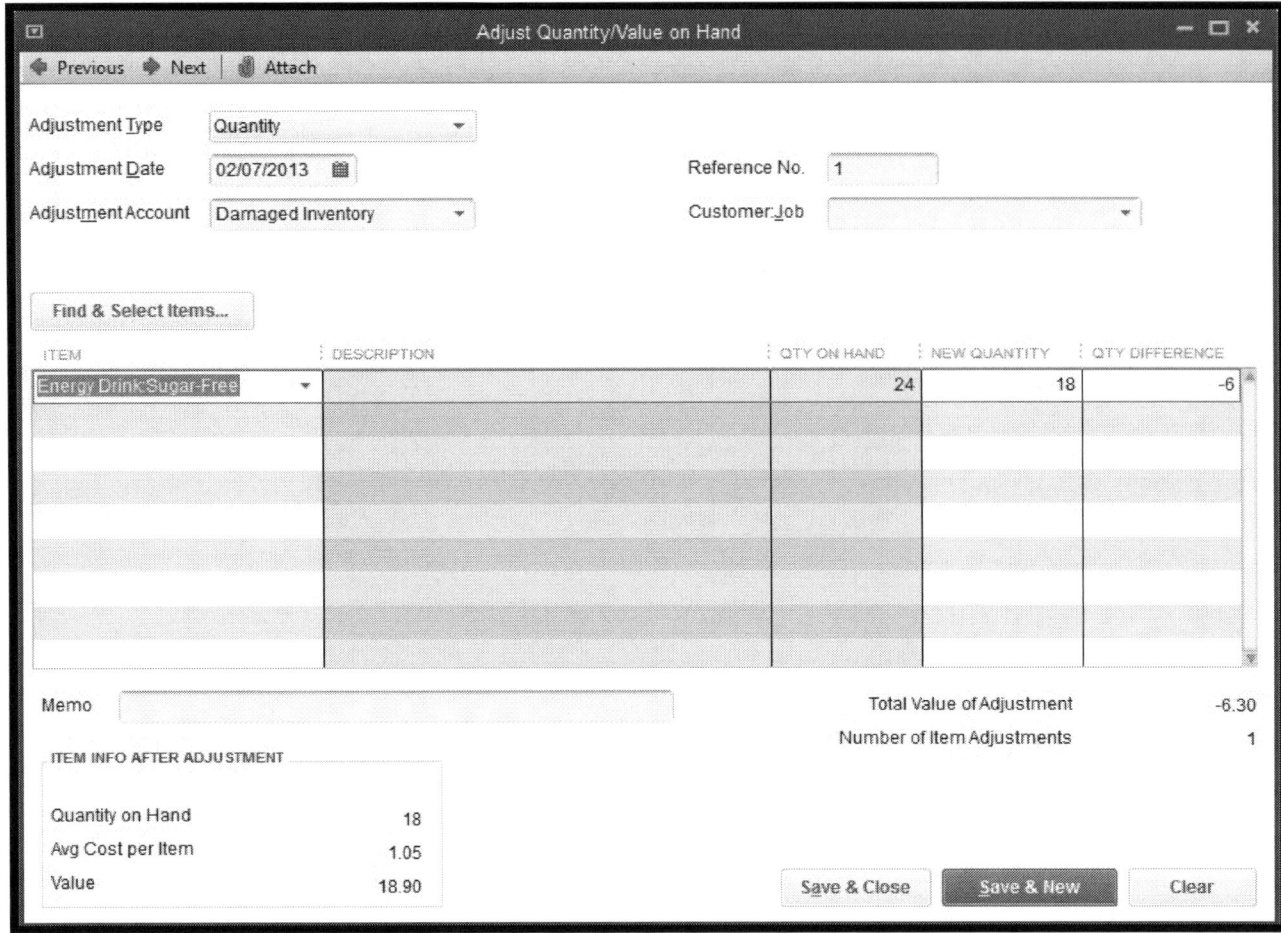

18. Feb 8: Check #1014 to Copper Property Management Co. in the amount of $1,500.00 for February rent.

19. Feb 10: Robert Markum paid $25 for a first time gym registration fee and a monthly membership fee of $35.

20. Feb 10: Sold 1 hour of personal training to Adrian Gonzalez for $35.

21. Feb 11: Received payment of $35 from Lucy Hopper for February gym membership (previously invoiced).

22. Feb 12: Charged $68.97 on Visa credit card at Wal-Mart for cleaning supplies (set up a new account).

23. Feb 12: Paid bill from Yoga Bliss, LLC (less 2% discount to a new income account Discount Earned) with Bill Payment Check #1015 in the amount of $230.30.

Note: Click on Set Discount to set up the Discount Earned account, also make sure to select assign check number.

QUICKBOOKS PRACTICE SET

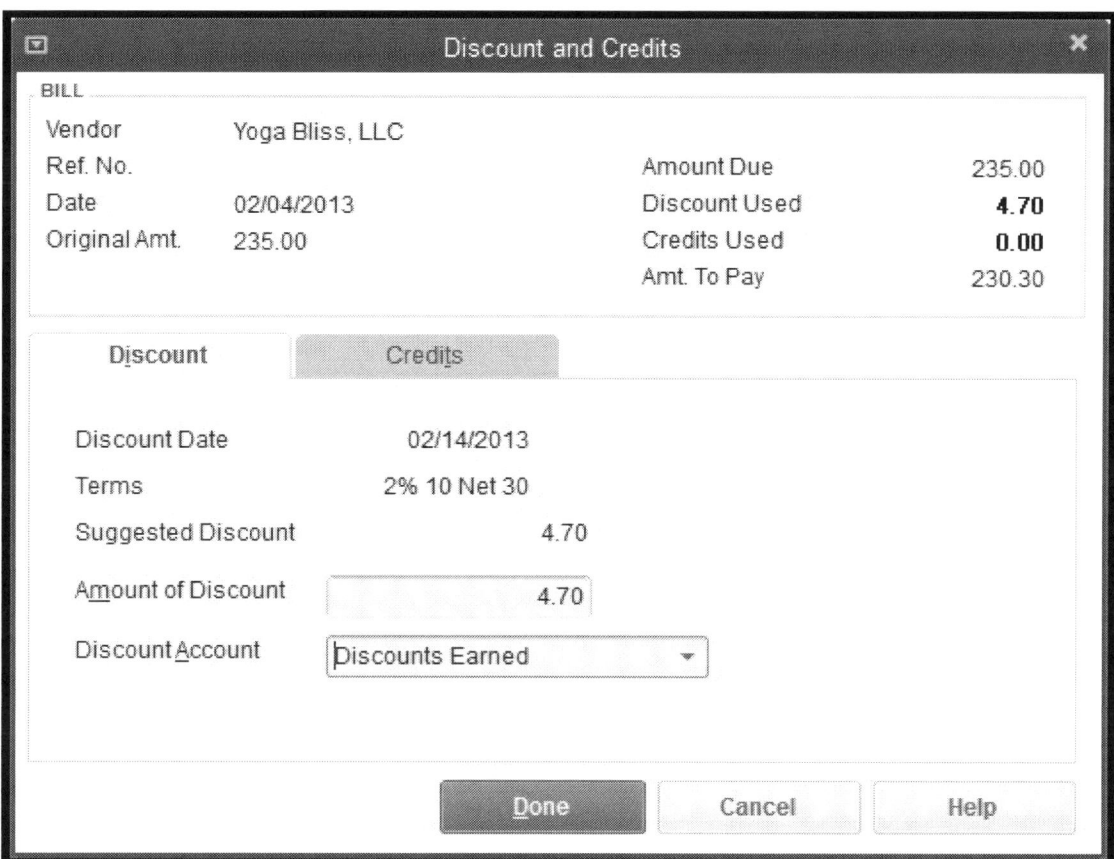

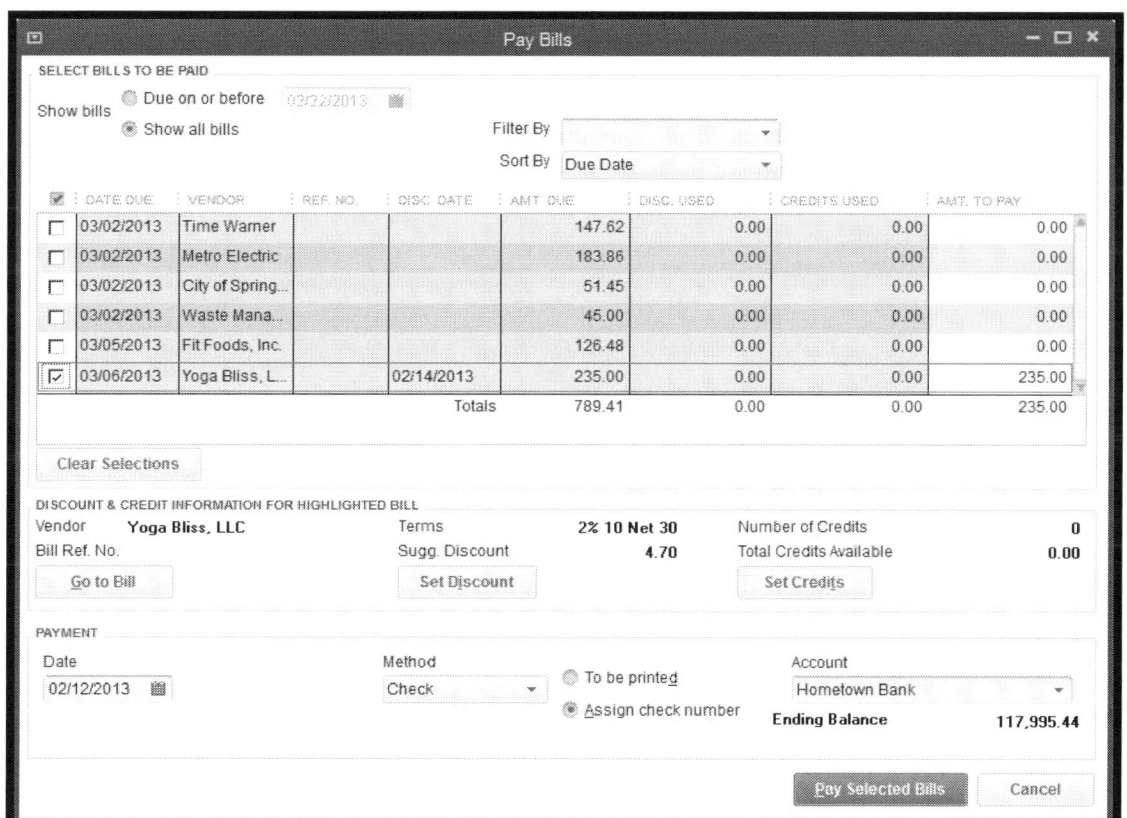

24. Feb 14: Julie Stein paid $90 for a quarterly (3 months) gym membership.

25. Feb 14: Total food sales from the week are shown in the table below:

Item	Quantity Sold	Sales Price	Totals
Bottled Water		$1.50	
Sports Drink:			
Lemon	3	2.00	$6.00
Orange		2.00	
Blue	2	2.00	4.00
Red	1	2.00	2.00
Energy Drink:			
Regular		3.75	
Sugar-Free	2	3.75	7.50
Nutrition Bar:			
Chocolate	3	3.25	9.75
Vanilla		3.25	
Peanut Butter		3.25	
Subtotal			**29.25**
Sales Tax			**2.34**
Total			**31.59**

26. Feb 14: Deposited all Undeposited funds from the second week of the month into the checking account. (Total Deposit $251.59)

27. Feb 14: Received payment of $35 from Daniel Brown for February gym membership (previously invoiced).

28. Feb 15: Issued a partial refund to Jim Hill for $20 because he sustained an injury and cannot use the rest of his month's gym membership.

Note: Under Refunds & Credits, enter the credit for the Item of Monthly. After you click to Save it, select Give a Refund to issue check #1016

29. Feb 16: Cindy Blackburn paid $25 for a first time gym registration fee and a monthly membership fee of $35. (Sales Receipt for $60)

30. Feb 18: Received bill from Swisher Marketing, LLC in the amount of $750.00 for direct mail marketing campaign with terms of 2/10, n/30. (Advertising and Promotion expense)

31. Feb 20: Christopher Tomlinson paid $25 for a first time gym registration fee and a monthly membership fee of $35.

32. Feb 21: Total food sales from the week are shown in the table below:

Item	Quantity Sold	Sales Price	Totals
Bottled Water	3	$1.50	$4.50
Sports Drink:			
Lemon		2.00	
Orange	1	2.00	2.00
Blue	4	2.00	8.00
Red		2.00	
Energy Drink:			
Regular		3.75	
Sugar-Free	3	3.75	11.25
Nutrition Bar:			
Chocolate	1	3.25	3.25
Vanilla	2	3.25	6.50
Peanut Butter	1	3.25	3.25
Subtotal			**38.75**
Sales Tax			**3.10**
Total			**41.85**

33. Feb 21: Deposited all Undeposited funds from the third week of the month into the checking account. Total Deposit is $196.85.

34. Feb 22: Sent invoices to the following members in the amount of $35 for March membership with terms of n/30:

    - Daniel Brown
    - Adrian Gonzalez
    - Lucy Steele
    - Jerry Kline
    - Tim Barnes
    - Robert Markum
    - Cindy Blackburn

    Note: Lucy Hopper, Jim Hill, and Christopher Tomlinson decided to not renew their membership.

35. Feb 23: Lynn Sampson paid $90 for a quarterly gym membership.

36. Feb 25: Paid bill in full from Swisher Marketing, LLC. (less 2% discount) in the amount of $735.00 with check #1017.

37. Feb 26: Sold 2 hours of personal training to Adrian Gonzalez for a total of $70.

38. Feb 28: Charged $56.70 on Visa credit card at Office Depot for printer ink.

39. Feb 28: Paid all outstanding bills. Total paid $554.41 and let QuickBooks assign check numbers 1018 through 1022.

40. Feb 28: Received bill from Time Warner in the amount of $147.62 for phone, internet, and cable services with terms of n/30.

41. Feb 28: Received bill from Metro Electric Co. in the amount of $178.86 for electricity with terms of n/30.

42. Feb 28: Received bill from City of Springfield in the amount of for $86.45 for water with terms of n/30.

43. Feb 28: Received bill from Waste Management in the amount of $45.00 for trash removal with terms of n/30.

44. Feb 28: Total food sales from the week are shown in the table below:

Item	Quantity Sold	Sales Price	Totals
Bottled Water	5	$1.50	$7.50
Sports Drink:			
Lemon	4	2.00	8.00
Orange	2	2.00	4.00
Blue	3	2.00	6.00
Red		2.00	
Energy Drink:			
Regular		3.75	
Sugar-Free	5	3.75	18.75
Nutrition Bar:			
Chocolate	2	3.25	6.50
Vanilla	3	3.25	9.75
Peanut Butter	1	3.25	3.25
Subtotal			**63.75**
Sales Tax			**5.10**
Total			**68.85**

45. Feb 28: Deposited all Undeposited funds from the last week of the month into the checking account. Total Deposit is $228.85.

Reconcile Accounts

Use the following information to reconcile the checking account:

Bank Statement Ending Date	2/28/2015
Bank Statement Ending Balance	$117,693.58
Outstanding Checks: Check # 1018 $51.45 Check # 1019 $126.48 Check # 1020 $183.86 Check # 1021 $147.62 Check # 1022 $45.00	Outstanding Deposits: 2/28/2015 $228.85

Use the following information to reconcile the Visa credit card account:

Bank Statement Ending Date	2/28/2015
Bank Statement Ending Balance	$68.97
Outstanding Items: Office Depot $56.70	

After reconciling the credit card account, select Write a check for payment now. Enter the payment date of Mar. 1 payable to Great American Bank for $68.97 with check number 1023.

QUICKBOOKS PRACTICE SET

Check Your Progress

Create the following reports and compare them to the following reports. (Make sure to change your dates for February only).

Balance Sheet

	Feb 28, 13
ASSETS	
Current Assets	
Checking/Savings	
Checking - Hometown Bank	117,368.02
Total Checking/Savings	117,368.02
Accounts Receivable	
Accounts Receivable	245.00
Total Accounts Receivable	245.00
Other Current Assets	
Inventory Asset	93.14
Total Other Current Assets	93.14
Total Current Assets	117,706.16
Fixed Assets	
Office Furniture and Equipment	4,123.15
Furniture and Equipment	81,200.00
Leasehold Improvements	52,736.89
Total Fixed Assets	138,060.04
Other Assets	
Security Deposits Assets	3,000.00
Total Other Assets	3,000.00
TOTAL ASSETS	258,766.20
LIABILITIES & EQUITY	
Liabilities	
Current Liabilities	

Accounts Payable		
Accounts Payable		457.93
Total Accounts Payable		457.93
Credit Cards		
Visa		125.67
Total Credit Cards		125.67
Other Current Liabilities		
Sales Tax Payable		11.44
Total Other Current Liabilities		11.44
Total Current Liabilities		595.04
Long Term Liabilities		
Note Payable - Hometown Bank		250,000.00
Total Long Term Liabilities		250,000.00
Total Liabilities		250,595.04
Equity		
Tom Martin		
Tom - Owner's Contribution		5,000.00
Total Tom Martin		5,000.00
Joe Watson		
Joe - Owner's Contributions		5,000.00
Total Joe Watson		5,000.00
Nancy Clemens		
Nancy - Owner's Contributions		5,000.00
Total Nancy Clemens		5,000.00
Net Income		-6,828.84
Total Equity		8,171.16
TOTAL LIABILITIES & EQUITY		258,766.20

QUICKBOOKS PRACTICE SET

Profit & Loss

	Jan 13	Feb 13	TOTAL
Ordinary Income/Expense			
Income			
Discounts Earned	0.00	19.70	19.70
Gym Fees	0.00	1,235.00	1,235.00
Merchandise Sales	0.00	143.00	143.00
Registration Fees	0.00	175.00	175.00
Total Income	0.00	1,572.70	1,572.70
Cost of Goods Sold			
Cost of Goods Sold	0.00	27.04	27.04
Total COGS	0.00	27.04	27.04
Gross Profit	0.00	1,545.66	1,545.66
Expense			
Cleaning Supplies	0.00	68.97	68.97
Damaged Inventory	0.00	6.30	6.30
Fitness Supplies	0.00	235.00	235.00
Advertising and Promotion	225.00	900.00	1,125.00
Computer and Internet Expenses	550.00	0.00	550.00
Office Supplies	136.67	56.70	193.37
Professional Fees			
Accounting Fees	0.00	450.00	450.00
Legal Fees	1,785.00	0.00	1,785.00
Total Professional Fees	1,785.00	450.00	2,235.00
Rent Expense	1,500.00	1,500.00	3,000.00
Repairs and Maintenance	0.00	75.00	75.00
Utilities			
Trash Removal	45.00	45.00	90.00
Water	51.45	86.45	137.90
Electricity	183.86	178.86	362.72
Phone and Internet	147.62	147.62	295.24
Total Utilities	427.93	457.93	885.86
Total Expense	4,624.60	3,749.90	8,374.50
Net Ordinary Income	-4,624.60	-2,204.24	-6,828.84
Net Income	-4,624.60	-2,204.24	-6,828.84

Accounts Receivable Aging Detail

	Type	Date	Num	Name	Terms	Due Date	Open Balance
Current							
	Invoice	02/22/2015	5	Brown, Daniel	Net 30	03/24/2015	35.00
	Invoice	02/22/2015	6	Gonzalez, Adrian	Net 30	03/24/2015	35.00
	Invoice	02/22/2015	7	Steele, Lucy	Net 30	03/24/2015	35.00
	Invoice	02/22/2015	8	Kline, Jerry	Net 30	03/24/2015	35.00
	Invoice	02/22/2015	9	Barnes, Tim	Net 30	03/24/2015	35.00
	Invoice	02/22/2015	10	Markum, Robert	Net 30	03/24/2015	35.00
	Invoice	02/22/2015	11	Blackburn, Cindy	Net 30	03/24/2015	35.00
Total Current							245.00

Accounts Payable Aging Detail

	Type	Date	Name	Due Date	Open Balance
Current					
	Bill	02/28/2015	Waste Management	03/30/2015	45.00
	Bill	02/28/2015	Time Warner	03/30/2015	147.62
	Bill	02/28/2015	Metro Electric Co.	03/30/2015	178.86
	Bill	02/28/2015	City of Springfield	03/30/2015	86.45
Total Current					457.93

Sales by Customer Detail

	Type	Date	Num	Item	Sales Price	Amount
Barnes, Tim						
	Sales Receipt	02/07/2015	10	Registration Fee	25.00	25.00
	Sales Receipt	02/07/2015	10	Monthly membership	35.00	35.00
	Sales Receipt	02/07/2015	12	Personal Training (Personal Training)	35.00	35.00
	Invoice	02/22/2015	8	Monthly membership	35.00	35.00
Total Barnes, Tim						130.00
Blackburn, Cindy						
	Sales Receipt	02/16/2015	17	Registration Fee	25.00	25.00
	Sales Receipt	02/16/2015	17	Monthly membership	35.00	35.00
	Invoice	02/22/2015	10	Monthly membership	35.00	35.00
Total Blackburn, Cindy						95.00
Brown, Daniel						
	Invoice	02/06/2015	2	Monthly membership	35.00	35.00
	Sales Receipt	02/07/2015	8	Wicked Weights	50.00	50.00
	Invoice	02/22/2015	5	Monthly membership	35.00	35.00
Total Brown, Daniel						120.00
Gonzalez, Adrian						
	Invoice	02/06/2015	1	Monthly membership	35.00	35.00
	Sales Receipt	02/07/2015	6	Basic Fitness 101	50.00	50.00
	Sales Receipt	02/10/2015	14	Personal Training (Personal Training)	35.00	35.00
	Invoice	02/22/2015	6	Monthly membership	35.00	35.00
	Sales Receipt	02/26/2015	21	Personal Training (Personal Training)	35.00	70.00
Total Gonzalez, Adrian						225.00
Gutierrez, Augusto						
	Sales Receipt	02/04/2015	4	Quarterly memberships	90.00	90.00
Total Gutierrez, Augusto						90.00
Hill, Jim						
	Sales Receipt	02/04/2015	3	Registration Fee	25.00	25.00
	Sales Receipt	02/04/2015	3	Monthly membership	35.00	35.00
	Sales Receipt	02/07/2015	9	Wicked Weights	50.00	50.00

	Credit Memo	02/15/2015	4	Monthly membership	20.00	-20.00
Total Hill, Jim						90.00

Hopper, Lucy

	Invoice	02/06/2015	3	Monthly membership	35.00	35.00
Total Hopper, Lucy						35.00

Kline, Jerry

	Sales Receipt	02/04/2015	2	Registration Fee	25.00	25.00
	Sales Receipt	02/04/2015	2	Monthly membership	35.00	35.00
	Sales Receipt	02/07/2015	5	Basic Fitness 101	50.00	50.00
	Invoice	02/22/2015	11	Monthly membership	35.00	35.00
Total Kline, Jerry						145.00

Markum, Robert

	Sales Receipt	02/10/2015	13	Registration Fee	25.00	25.00
	Sales Receipt	02/10/2015	13	Monthly membership	35.00	35.00
	Invoice	02/22/2015	9	Monthly membership	35.00	35.00
Total Markum, Robert						95.00

Sampson, Lynn

	Sales Receipt	02/23/2015	20	Quarterly memberships	90.00	90.00
Total Sampson, Lynn						90.00

Steele, Lucy

	Sales Receipt	02/04/2015	1	Registration Fee	25.00	25.00
	Sales Receipt	02/04/2015	1	Monthly membership	35.00	35.00
	Sales Receipt	02/07/2015	7	Basic Fitness 101	50.00	50.00
	Invoice	02/22/2015	7	Monthly membership	35.00	35.00
Total Steele, Lucy						145.00

Stein, Julie

	Sales Receipt	02/14/2015	15	Quarterly memberships	90.00	90.00
Total Stein, Julie						90.00

Tomlinson, Christopher

	Sales Receipt	02/20/2015	18	Registration Fee	25.00	25.00
	Sales Receipt	02/20/2015	18	Monthly membership	35.00	35.00
Total Tomlinson, Christopher						60.00

Weekly Sales

Sales Receipt	02/07/2015	11	Sports Drink:Orange		2.00	4.00
Sales Receipt	02/07/2015	11	Sports Drink:Blue		2.00	4.00
Sales Receipt	02/07/2015	11	Nutrition Bar:Chocolate		3.25	3.25
Sales Receipt	02/14/2015	16	Sports Drink:Lemon		2.00	6.00
Sales Receipt	02/14/2015	16	Sports Drink:Blue		2.00	4.00
Sales Receipt	02/14/2015	16	Sports Drink:Red		2.00	2.00
Sales Receipt	02/14/2015	16	Energy Drink:Sugar-Free		3.75	7.50
Sales Receipt	02/14/2015	16	Nutrition Bar:Chocolate		3.25	9.75
Sales Receipt	02/21/2015	19	Bottled Water		1.50	4.50
Sales Receipt	02/21/2015	19	Sports Drink:Orange		2.00	2.00
Sales Receipt	02/21/2015	19	Sports Drink:Blue		2.00	8.00
Sales Receipt	02/21/2015	19	Energy Drink:Sugar-Free		3.75	11.25
Sales Receipt	02/21/2015	19	Nutrition Bar:Chocolate		3.25	3.25
Sales Receipt	02/21/2015	19	Nutrition Bar:Vanilla		3.25	6.50
Sales Receipt	02/21/2015	19	Nutrition Bar:Peanut Butter		3.25	3.25
Sales Receipt	02/28/2015	22	Bottled Water		1.50	7.50
Sales Receipt	02/28/2015	22	Sports Drink:Lemon		2.00	8.00
Sales Receipt	02/28/2015	22	Sports Drink:Orange		2.00	4.00
Sales Receipt	02/28/2015	22	Sports Drink:Blue		2.00	6.00
Sales Receipt	02/28/2015	22	Energy Drink:Sugar-Free		3.75	18.75
Sales Receipt	02/28/2015	22	Nutrition Bar:Chocolate		3.25	6.50
Sales Receipt	02/28/2015	22	Nutrition Bar:Vanilla		3.25	9.75
Sales Receipt	02/28/2015	22	Nutrition Bar:Peanut Butter		3.25	3.25

Total Weekly Sales   **143.00**

1,553.00

Sales by Item Detail

	Type	Date	Name	Qty	Sales Price	Amount
Inventory						
Bottled Water						
	Sales Receipt	02/21/2015	Weekly Sales	3.00	1.50	4.50
	Sales Receipt	02/28/2015	Weekly Sales	5.00	1.50	7.50
Total Bottled Water				8.00		12.00
Energy Drink						
Sugar-Free						
	Sales Receipt	02/14/2015	Weekly Sales	2.00	3.75	7.50
	Sales Receipt	02/21/2015	Weekly Sales	3.00	3.75	11.25
	Sales Receipt	02/28/2015	Weekly Sales	5.00	3.75	18.75
Total Sugar-Free				10.00		37.50
Total Energy Drink				10.00		37.50
Nutrition Bar						
Chocolate						
	Sales Receipt	02/07/2015	Weekly Sales	1.00	3.25	3.25
	Sales Receipt	02/14/2015	Weekly Sales	3.00	3.25	9.75
	Sales Receipt	02/21/2015	Weekly Sales	1.00	3.25	3.25
	Sales Receipt	02/28/2015	Weekly Sales	2.00	3.25	6.50
Total Chocolate				7.00		22.75
Peanut Butter						
	Sales Receipt	02/21/2015	Weekly Sales	1.00	3.25	3.25
	Sales Receipt	02/28/2015	Weekly Sales	1.00	3.25	3.25
Total Peanut Butter				2.00		6.50
Vanilla						
	Sales Receipt	02/21/2015	Weekly Sales	2.00	3.25	6.50
	Sales Receipt	02/28/2015	Weekly Sales	3.00	3.25	9.75
Total Vanilla				5.00		16.25
Total Nutrition Bar				14.00		45.50

Sports Drink

   Blue

	Sales Receipt	02/07/2015	Weekly Sales	2.00	2.00	4.00
	Sales Receipt	02/14/2015	Weekly Sales	2.00	2.00	4.00
	Sales Receipt	02/21/2015	Weekly Sales	4.00	2.00	8.00
	Sales Receipt	02/28/2015	Weekly Sales	3.00	2.00	6.00
Total Blue				11.00		22.00

   Lemon

	Sales Receipt	02/14/2015	Weekly Sales	3.00	2.00	6.00
	Sales Receipt	02/28/2015	Weekly Sales	4.00	2.00	8.00
Total Lemon				7.00		14.00

   Orange

	Sales Receipt	02/07/2015	Weekly Sales	2.00	2.00	4.00
	Sales Receipt	02/21/2015	Weekly Sales	1.00	2.00	2.00
	Sales Receipt	02/28/2015	Weekly Sales	2.00	2.00	4.00
Total Orange				5.00		10.00

   Red

	Sales Receipt	02/14/2015	Weekly Sales	1.00	2.00	2.00
Total Red				1.00		2.00

Total Sports Drink   24.00   48.00

Total Inventory   56.00   143.00

Service

   Basic Fitness 101

	Sales Receipt	02/07/2015	Kline, Jerry	1.00	50.00	50.00
	Sales Receipt	02/07/2015	Gonzalez, Adrian	1.00	50.00	50.00
	Sales Receipt	02/07/2015	Steele, Lucy	1.00	50.00	50.00
Total Basic Fitness 101				3.00		150.00

   Monthly membership

	Sales Receipt	02/04/2015	Steele, Lucy	1.00	35.00	35.00
	Sales Receipt	02/04/2015	Kline, Jerry	1.00	35.00	35.00
	Sales Receipt	02/04/2015	Hill, Jim	1.00	35.00	35.00
	Invoice	02/06/2015	Gonzalez, Adrian	1.00	35.00	35.00

	Invoice	02/06/2015	Brown, Daniel	1.00	35.00	35.00
	Invoice	02/06/2015	Hopper, Lucy	1.00	35.00	35.00
	Sales Receipt	02/07/2015	Barnes, Tim	1.00	35.00	35.00
	Sales Receipt	02/10/2015	Markum, Robert	1.00	35.00	35.00
	Credit Memo	02/15/2015	Hill, Jim	-1.00	20.00	-20.00
	Sales Receipt	02/16/2015	Blackburn, Cindy	1.00	35.00	35.00
	Sales Receipt	02/20/2015	Tomlinson, Christopher	1.00	35.00	35.00
	Invoice	02/22/2015	Brown, Daniel	1.00	35.00	35.00
	Invoice	02/22/2015	Gonzalez, Adrian	1.00	35.00	35.00
	Invoice	02/22/2015	Steele, Lucy	1.00	35.00	35.00
	Invoice	02/22/2015	Barnes, Tim	1.00	35.00	35.00
	Invoice	02/22/2015	Markum, Robert	1.00	35.00	35.00
	Invoice	02/22/2015	Blackburn, Cindy	1.00	35.00	35.00
	Invoice	02/22/2015	Kline, Jerry	1.00	35.00	35.00
Total Monthly membership				16.00		575.00

Personal Training (Personal Training)

	Sales Receipt	02/07/2015	Barnes, Tim	1.00	35.00	35.00
	Sales Receipt	02/10/2015	Gonzalez, Adrian	1.00	35.00	35.00
	Sales Receipt	02/26/2015	Gonzalez, Adrian	2.00	35.00	70.00
Total Personal Training (Personal Training)				4.00		140.00

Quarterly memberships

	Sales Receipt	02/04/2015	Gutierrez, Augusto	1.00	90.00	90.00
	Sales Receipt	02/14/2015	Stein, Julie	1.00	90.00	90.00
	Sales Receipt	02/23/2015	Sampson, Lynn	1.00	90.00	90.00
Total Quarterly memberships				3.00		270.00

Registration Fee

	Sales Receipt	02/04/2015	Steele, Lucy	1.00	25.00	25.00
	Sales Receipt	02/04/2015	Kline, Jerry	1.00	25.00	25.00
	Sales Receipt	02/04/2015	Hill, Jim	1.00	25.00	25.00
	Sales Receipt	02/07/2015	Barnes, Tim	1.00	25.00	25.00
	Sales Receipt	02/10/2015	Markum, Robert	1.00	25.00	25.00
	Sales Receipt	02/16/2015	Blackburn, Cindy	1.00	25.00	25.00
	Sales Receipt	02/20/2015	Tomlinson, Christopher	1.00	25.00	25.00
Total Registration Fee				7.00		175.00

QUICKBOOKS PRACTICE SET

Wicked Weights

	Sales Receipt	02/07/2015	Brown, Daniel	1.00	50.00	50.00
	Sales Receipt	02/07/2015	Hill, Jim	1.00	50.00	50.00
Total Wicked Weights				2.00		100.00
Total Service				35.00		1,410.00
				91.00		**1,553.00**

Inventory Stock Status by Item

	On Hand	On PO	Next Deliv	Sales/Week
Inventory				
Bottled Water	40.00	0.00		2.00
Energy Drink				
Regular	24.00	0.00		0.00
Sugar-Free	8.00	0.00		2.50
Energy Drink - Other	0.00	0.00		0.00
Total Energy Drink	32.00	0.00		2.50
Nutrition Bar				
Chocolate	17.00	0.00		1.80
Peanut Butter	22.00	0.00		0.50
Vanilla	19.00	0.00		1.30
Nutrition Bar - Other	0.00	0.00		0.00
Total Nutrition Bar	58.00	0.00		3.60
Sports Drink				
Blue	13.00	0.00		2.80
Lemon	17.00	0.00		1.80
Orange	19.00	0.00		1.30
Red	23.00	0.00		0.30
Sports Drink - Other	0.00	0.00		0.00
Total Sports Drink	72.00	0.00		6.20

Transaction List by Date

Type	Date	Num	Name	Account	Split	Debit	Credit
Check	02/01/2015	1010	Great American Bank	Hometown Bank	Visa		1,859.82
Check	02/01/2015	1010	Great American Bank	Visa	Hometown Bank	1,859.82	
Check	02/01/2015	1011	Oak Hill Homeowners Association	Hometown Bank	Advertising and Promotion		150.00
Check	02/01/2015	1011	Oak Hill Homeowners Association	Advertising and Promotion	Hometown Bank	150.00	
Check	02/03/2015	1012	Willy's Windows	Hometown Bank	Repairs and Maintenance		75.00
Check	02/03/2015	1012	Willy's Windows	Repairs and Maintenance	Hometown Bank	75.00	
Bill	02/03/2015		Fit Foods, Inc.	Accounts Payable	-SPLIT-		126.48
Bill	02/03/2015		Fit Foods, Inc.	Inventory Asset	Accounts Payable	8.16	
Bill	02/03/2015		Fit Foods, Inc.	Inventory Asset	Accounts Payable	8.88	
Bill	02/03/2015		Fit Foods, Inc.	Inventory Asset	Accounts Payable	8.88	
Bill	02/03/2015		Fit Foods, Inc.	Inventory Asset	Accounts Payable	8.88	
Bill	02/03/2015		Fit Foods, Inc.	Inventory Asset	Accounts Payable	8.88	
Bill	02/03/2015		Fit Foods, Inc.	Inventory Asset	Accounts Payable	25.20	
Bill	02/03/2015		Fit Foods, Inc.	Inventory Asset	Accounts Payable	25.20	
Bill	02/03/2015		Fit Foods, Inc.	Inventory Asset	Accounts Payable	10.80	
Bill	02/03/2015		Fit Foods, Inc.	Inventory Asset	Accounts Payable	10.80	
Bill	02/03/2015		Fit Foods, Inc.	Inventory Asset	Accounts Payable	10.80	
Sales Receipt	02/04/2015	1	Steele, Lucy	Undeposited Funds	-SPLIT-	60.00	
Sales Receipt	02/04/2015	1	Steele, Lucy	Registration Fees	Undeposited Funds		25.00
Sales Receipt	02/04/2015	1	Steele, Lucy	Gym Revenues	Undeposited Funds		35.00
Sales Receipt	02/04/2015	1	Steele, Lucy	Sales Tax Payable	Undeposited Funds	0.00	
Sales Receipt	02/04/2015	2	Kline, Jerry	Undeposited Funds	-SPLIT-	60.00	
Sales Receipt	02/04/2015	2	Kline, Jerry	Registration Fees	Undeposited Funds		25.00
Sales Receipt	02/04/2015	2	Kline, Jerry	Gym Revenues	Undeposited Funds		35.00
Sales Receipt	02/04/2015	2	Kline, Jerry	Sales Tax Payable	Undeposited Funds	0.00	
Bill	02/04/2015		Yoga Bliss, LLC	Accounts Payable	Fitness Supplies		235.00
Bill	02/04/2015		Yoga Bliss, LLC	Fitness Supplies	Accounts Payable	235.00	
Sales Receipt	02/04/2015	3	Hill, Jim	Undeposited Funds	-SPLIT-	60.00	
Sales Receipt	02/04/2015	3	Hill, Jim	Registration Fees	Undeposited Funds		25.00
Sales Receipt	02/04/2015	3	Hill, Jim	Gym Revenues	Undeposited Funds		35.00
Sales Receipt	02/04/2015	3	Hill, Jim	Sales Tax Payable	Undeposited Funds	0.00	
Sales Receipt	02/04/2015	4	Gutierrez, Augusto	Undeposited Funds	-SPLIT-	90.00	
Sales Receipt	02/04/2015	4	Gutierrez, Augusto	Gym Revenues	Undeposited Funds		90.00
Sales Receipt	02/04/2015	4	Gutierrez, Augusto	Sales Tax Payable	Undeposited Funds	0.00	

Type	Date	Num	Name	Account	Split	Debit	Credit
Check	02/05/2015	1013	Long for Success, LLC	Hometown Bank	Accounting Fees		450.00
Check	02/05/2015	1013	Long for Success, LLC	Accounting Fees	Hometown Bank	450.00	
Invoice	02/06/2015	1	Gonzalez, Adrian	Accounts Receivable	-SPLIT-	35.00	
Invoice	02/06/2015	1	Gonzalez, Adrian	Gym Revenues	Accounts Receivable		35.00
Invoice	02/06/2015	1	Gonzalez, Adrian	Sales Tax Payable	Accounts Receivable	0.00	
Invoice	02/06/2015	2	Brown, Daniel	Accounts Receivable	-SPLIT-	35.00	
Invoice	02/06/2015	2	Brown, Daniel	Gym Revenues	Accounts Receivable		35.00
Invoice	02/06/2015	2	Brown, Daniel	Sales Tax Payable	Accounts Receivable	0.00	
Invoice	02/06/2015	3	Hopper, Lucy	Accounts Receivable	-SPLIT-	35.00	
Invoice	02/06/2015	3	Hopper, Lucy	Gym Revenues	Accounts Receivable		35.00
Invoice	02/06/2015	3	Hopper, Lucy	Sales Tax Payable	Accounts Receivable	0.00	
Sales Receipt	02/07/2015	5	Kline, Jerry	Undeposited Funds	-SPLIT-	50.00	
Sales Receipt	02/07/2015	5	Kline, Jerry	Gym Revenues	Undeposited Funds		50.00
Sales Receipt	02/07/2015	5	Kline, Jerry	Sales Tax Payable	Undeposited Funds	0.00	
Sales Receipt	02/07/2015	6	Gonzalez, Adrian	Undeposited Funds	-SPLIT-	50.00	
Sales Receipt	02/07/2015	6	Gonzalez, Adrian	Gym Revenues	Undeposited Funds		50.00
Sales Receipt	02/07/2015	6	Gonzalez, Adrian	Sales Tax Payable	Undeposited Funds	0.00	
Sales Receipt	02/07/2015	7	Steele, Lucy	Undeposited Funds	-SPLIT-	50.00	
Sales Receipt	02/07/2015	7	Steele, Lucy	Gym Revenues	Undeposited Funds		50.00
Sales Receipt	02/07/2015	7	Steele, Lucy	Sales Tax Payable	Undeposited Funds	0.00	
Sales Receipt	02/07/2015	8	Brown, Daniel	Undeposited Funds	-SPLIT-	50.00	
Sales Receipt	02/07/2015	8	Brown, Daniel	Gym Revenues	Undeposited Funds		50.00
Sales Receipt	02/07/2015	8	Brown, Daniel	Sales Tax Payable	Undeposited Funds	0.00	
Sales Receipt	02/07/2015	9	Hill, Jim	Undeposited Funds	-SPLIT-	50.00	
Sales Receipt	02/07/2015	9	Hill, Jim	Gym Revenues	Undeposited Funds		50.00
Sales Receipt	02/07/2015	9	Hill, Jim	Sales Tax Payable	Undeposited Funds	0.00	
Sales Receipt	02/07/2015	10	Barnes, Tim	Undeposited Funds	-SPLIT-	60.00	
Sales Receipt	02/07/2015	10	Barnes, Tim	Registration Fees	Undeposited Funds		25.00
Sales Receipt	02/07/2015	10	Barnes, Tim	Gym Revenues	Undeposited Funds		35.00
Sales Receipt	02/07/2015	10	Barnes, Tim	Sales Tax Payable	Undeposited Funds	0.00	
Payment	02/07/2015		Gonzalez, Adrian	Undeposited Funds	Accounts Receivable	35.00	
Payment	02/07/2015		Gonzalez, Adrian	Accounts Receivable	Undeposited Funds		35.00
Sales Receipt	02/07/2015	11	Weekly Sales	Undeposited Funds	-SPLIT-	12.15	
Sales Receipt	02/07/2015	11	Weekly Sales	Merchandise Sales	Undeposited Funds		4.00
Sales Receipt	02/07/2015	11	Weekly Sales	Inventory Asset	Undeposited Funds		0.74
Sales Receipt	02/07/2015	11	Weekly Sales	Cost of Goods Sold	Undeposited Funds	0.74	
Sales Receipt	02/07/2015	11	Weekly Sales	Merchandise Sales	Undeposited Funds		4.00
Sales Receipt	02/07/2015	11	Weekly Sales	Inventory Asset	Undeposited		0.74

QUICKBOOKS PRACTICE SET

Sales Receipt	02/07/2015	11	Weekly Sales	Cost of Goods Sold	Undeposited Funds	0.74	
Sales Receipt	02/07/2015	11	Weekly Sales	Merchandise Sales	Undeposited Funds		3.25
Sales Receipt	02/07/2015	11	Weekly Sales	Inventory Asset	Undeposited Funds		0.45
Sales Receipt	02/07/2015	11	Weekly Sales	Cost of Goods Sold	Undeposited Funds	0.45	
Sales Receipt	02/07/2015	11	Iowa Department of Revenue	Sales Tax Payable	Undeposited Funds		0.90
Sales Receipt	02/07/2015	12	Barnes, Tim	Undeposited Funds	-SPLIT-	35.00	
Sales Receipt	02/07/2015	12	Barnes, Tim	Gym Revenues	Undeposited Funds		35.00
Sales Receipt	02/07/2015	12	Barnes, Tim	Sales Tax Payable	Undeposited Funds	0.00	
Deposit	02/07/2015			Hometown Bank	-SPLIT-	662.15	
Deposit	02/07/2015		Steele, Lucy	Undeposited Funds	Hometown Bank		60.00
Deposit	02/07/2015		Kline, Jerry	Undeposited Funds	Hometown Bank		60.00
Deposit	02/07/2015		Hill, Jim	Undeposited Funds	Hometown Bank		60.00
Deposit	02/07/2015		Gutierrez, Augusto	Undeposited Funds	Hometown Bank		90.00
Deposit	02/07/2015		Kline, Jerry	Undeposited Funds	Hometown Bank		50.00
Deposit	02/07/2015		Gonzalez, Adrian	Undeposited Funds	Hometown Bank		50.00
Deposit	02/07/2015		Steele, Lucy	Undeposited Funds	Hometown Bank		50.00
Deposit	02/07/2015		Brown, Daniel	Undeposited Funds	Hometown Bank		50.00
Deposit	02/07/2015		Hill, Jim	Undeposited Funds	Hometown Bank		50.00
Deposit	02/07/2015		Barnes, Tim	Undeposited Funds	Hometown Bank		60.00
Deposit	02/07/2015		Gonzalez, Adrian	Undeposited Funds	Hometown Bank		35.00
Deposit	02/07/2015		Weekly Sales	Undeposited Funds	Hometown Bank		12.15
Deposit	02/07/2015		Barnes, Tim	Undeposited Funds	Hometown Bank		35.00
Inventory Adjust	02/07/2015	1		Damaged Inventory	Inventory Asset	6.30	
Inventory Adjust	02/07/2015	1		Inventory Asset	Damaged Inventory		6.30
Check	02/08/2015	1014	Copper Property Management Co	Hometown Bank	Rent Expense		1,500.00
Check	02/08/2015	1014	Copper Property Management Co	Rent Expense	Hometown Bank	1,500.00	
Sales Receipt	02/10/2015	13	Markum, Robert	Undeposited Funds	-SPLIT-	60.00	
Sales Receipt	02/10/2015	13	Markum, Robert	Registration Fees	Undeposited Funds		25.00
Sales Receipt	02/10/2015	13	Markum, Robert	Gym Revenues	Undeposited Funds		35.00
Sales Receipt	02/10/2015	13	Markum, Robert	Sales Tax Payable	Undeposited Funds	0.00	
Sales Receipt	02/10/2015	14	Gonzalez, Adrian	Undeposited Funds	-SPLIT-	35.00	
Sales Receipt	02/10/2015	14	Gonzalez, Adrian	Gym Revenues	Undeposited Funds		35.00
Sales Receipt	02/10/2015	14	Gonzalez, Adrian	Sales Tax Payable	Undeposited Funds	0.00	
Payment	02/11/2015		Hopper, Lucy	Undeposited Funds	Accounts Receivable	35.00	
Payment	02/11/2015		Hopper, Lucy	Accounts Receivable	Undeposited Funds		35.00
Credit Card Charge	02/12/2015		Wal-Mart	Visa	Cleaning Supplies		68.97
Credit Card Charge	02/12/2015		Wal-Mart	Cleaning Supplies	Visa	68.97	
Bill Pmt - Check	02/12/2015	1015	Yoga Bliss, LLC	Hometown Bank	-SPLIT-		230.30

MICHELLE L. LONG AND ANDREW S. LONG

Type	Date	Num	Name	Account	Split	Debit	Credit
Bill Pmt - Check	02/12/2015	1015	Yoga Bliss, LLC	Accounts Payable	Hometown Bank	230.30	
Discount	02/12/2015	1015	Yoga Bliss, LLC	Accounts Payable	Hometown Bank	4.70	
Bill Pmt - Check	02/12/2015	1015	Yoga Bliss, LLC	Discounts Earned	Hometown Bank		4.70
Sales Receipt	02/14/2015	15	Stein, Julie	Undeposited Funds	-SPLIT-	90.00	
Sales Receipt	02/14/2015	15	Stein, Julie	Gym Revenues	Undeposited Funds		90.00
Sales Receipt	02/14/2015	15	Stein, Julie	Sales Tax Payable	Undeposited Funds		0.00
Sales Receipt	02/14/2015	16	Weekly Sales	Undeposited Funds	-SPLIT-	31.59	
Sales Receipt	02/14/2015	16	Weekly Sales	Merchandise Sales	Undeposited Funds		6.00
Sales Receipt	02/14/2015	16	Weekly Sales	Inventory Asset	Undeposited Funds		1.11
Sales Receipt	02/14/2015	16	Weekly Sales	Cost of Goods Sold	Undeposited Funds	1.11	
Sales Receipt	02/14/2015	16	Weekly Sales	Merchandise Sales	Undeposited Funds		4.00
Sales Receipt	02/14/2015	16	Weekly Sales	Inventory Asset	Undeposited Funds		0.74
Sales Receipt	02/14/2015	16	Weekly Sales	Cost of Goods Sold	Undeposited Funds	0.74	
Sales Receipt	02/14/2015	16	Weekly Sales	Merchandise Sales	Undeposited Funds		2.00
Sales Receipt	02/14/2015	16	Weekly Sales	Inventory Asset	Undeposited Funds		0.37
Sales Receipt	02/14/2015	16	Weekly Sales	Cost of Goods Sold	Undeposited Funds	0.37	
Sales Receipt	02/14/2015	16	Weekly Sales	Merchandise Sales	Undeposited Funds		7.50
Sales Receipt	02/14/2015	16	Weekly Sales	Inventory Asset	Undeposited Funds		2.10
Sales Receipt	02/14/2015	16	Weekly Sales	Cost of Goods Sold	Undeposited Funds	2.10	
Sales Receipt	02/14/2015	16	Weekly Sales	Merchandise Sales	Undeposited Funds		9.75
Sales Receipt	02/14/2015	16	Weekly Sales	Inventory Asset	Undeposited Funds		1.35
Sales Receipt	02/14/2015	16	Weekly Sales	Cost of Goods Sold	Undeposited Funds	1.35	
Sales Receipt	02/14/2015	16	Iowa Department of Revenue	Sales Tax Payable	Undeposited Funds		2.34
Deposit	02/14/2015			Hometown Bank	-SPLIT-	251.59	
Deposit	02/14/2015		Markum, Robert	Undeposited Funds	Hometown Bank		60.00
Deposit	02/14/2015		Gonzalez, Adrian	Undeposited Funds	Hometown Bank		35.00
Deposit	02/14/2015		Hopper, Lucy	Undeposited Funds	Hometown Bank		35.00
Deposit	02/14/2015		Stein, Julie	Undeposited Funds	Hometown Bank		90.00
Deposit	02/14/2015		Weekly Sales	Undeposited Funds	Hometown Bank		31.59
Payment	02/14/2015		Brown, Daniel	Undeposited Funds	Accounts Receivable	35.00	
Payment	02/14/2015		Brown, Daniel	Accounts Receivable	Undeposited Funds		35.00
Credit Memo	02/15/2015	4	Hill, Jim	Accounts Receivable	-SPLIT-	20.00	
Credit Memo	02/15/2015	4	Hill, Jim	Gym Revenues	Accounts Receivable	20.00	
Credit Memo	02/15/2015	4	Hill, Jim	Sales Tax Payable	Accounts Receivable	0.00	
Check	02/15/2015	1016	Hill, Jim	Hometown Bank	Accounts Receivable		20.00
Check	02/15/2015	1016	Hill, Jim	Accounts Receivable	Hometown Bank	20.00	
Sales Receipt	02/16/2015	17	Blackburn, Cindy	Undeposited Funds	-SPLIT-	60.00	
Sales Receipt	02/16/2015	17	Blackburn, Cindy	Registration Fees	Undeposited Funds		25.00

QUICKBOOKS PRACTICE SET

Type	Date	Num	Name	Account	Split	Debit	Credit
Sales Receipt	02/16/2015	17	Blackburn, Cindy	Gym Revenues	Undeposited Funds		35.00
Sales Receipt	02/16/2015	17	Blackburn, Cindy	Sales Tax Payable	Undeposited Funds		0.00
Bill	02/18/2015		Swisher Marketing, LLC	Accounts Payable	Advertising and Promotion		750.00
Bill	02/18/2015		Swisher Marketing, LLC	Advertising and Promotion	Accounts Payable	750.00	
Sales Receipt	02/20/2015	18	Tomlinson, Christopher	Undeposited Funds	-SPLIT-	60.00	
Sales Receipt	02/20/2015	18	Tomlinson, Christopher	Registration Fees	Undeposited Funds		25.00
Sales Receipt	02/20/2015	18	Tomlinson, Christopher	Gym Revenues	Undeposited Funds		35.00
Sales Receipt	02/20/2015	18	Tomlinson, Christopher	Sales Tax Payable	Undeposited Funds		0.00
Sales Receipt	02/21/2015	19	Weekly Sales	Undeposited Funds	-SPLIT-	41.85	
Sales Receipt	02/21/2015	19	Weekly Sales	Merchandise Sales	Undeposited Funds		4.50
Sales Receipt	02/21/2015	19	Weekly Sales	Inventory Asset	Undeposited Funds		0.51
Sales Receipt	02/21/2015	19	Weekly Sales	Cost of Goods Sold	Undeposited Funds	0.51	
Sales Receipt	02/21/2015	19	Weekly Sales	Merchandise Sales	Undeposited Funds		2.00
Sales Receipt	02/21/2015	19	Weekly Sales	Inventory Asset	Undeposited Funds		0.37
Sales Receipt	02/21/2015	19	Weekly Sales	Cost of Goods Sold	Undeposited Funds	0.37	
Sales Receipt	02/21/2015	19	Weekly Sales	Merchandise Sales	Undeposited Funds		8.00
Sales Receipt	02/21/2015	19	Weekly Sales	Inventory Asset	Undeposited Funds		1.48
Sales Receipt	02/21/2015	19	Weekly Sales	Cost of Goods Sold	Undeposited Funds	1.48	
Sales Receipt	02/21/2015	19	Weekly Sales	Merchandise Sales	Undeposited Funds		11.25
Sales Receipt	02/21/2015	19	Weekly Sales	Inventory Asset	Undeposited Funds		3.15
Sales Receipt	02/21/2015	19	Weekly Sales	Cost of Goods Sold	Undeposited Funds	3.15	
Sales Receipt	02/21/2015	19	Weekly Sales	Merchandise Sales	Undeposited Funds		3.25
Sales Receipt	02/21/2015	19	Weekly Sales	Inventory Asset	Undeposited Funds		0.45
Sales Receipt	02/21/2015	19	Weekly Sales	Cost of Goods Sold	Undeposited Funds	0.45	
Sales Receipt	02/21/2015	19	Weekly Sales	Merchandise Sales	Undeposited Funds		6.50
Sales Receipt	02/21/2015	19	Weekly Sales	Inventory Asset	Undeposited Funds		0.90
Sales Receipt	02/21/2015	19	Weekly Sales	Cost of Goods Sold	Undeposited Funds	0.90	
Sales Receipt	02/21/2015	19	Weekly Sales	Merchandise Sales	Undeposited Funds		3.25
Sales Receipt	02/21/2015	19	Weekly Sales	Inventory Asset	Undeposited Funds		0.45
Sales Receipt	02/21/2015	19	Weekly Sales	Cost of Goods Sold	Undeposited Funds	0.45	
Sales Receipt	02/21/2015	19	Iowa Department of Revenue	Sales Tax Payable	Undeposited Funds		3.10
Deposit	02/21/2015			Hometown Bank	-SPLIT-	196.85	
Deposit	02/21/2015		Brown, Daniel	Undeposited Funds	Hometown Bank		35.00
Deposit	02/21/2015		Blackburn, Cindy	Undeposited Funds	Hometown Bank		60.00
Deposit	02/21/2015		Tomlinson, Christopher	Undeposited Funds	Hometown Bank		60.00
Deposit	02/21/2015		Weekly Sales	Undeposited Funds	Hometown Bank		41.85
Invoice	02/22/2015	5	Brown, Daniel	Accounts Receivable	-SPLIT-	35.00	

MICHELLE L. LONG AND ANDREW S. LONG

Type	Date	Num	Name	Account	Split	Debit	Credit
Invoice	02/22/2015	5	Brown, Daniel	Gym Revenues	Accounts Receivable		35.00
Invoice	02/22/2015	5	Brown, Daniel	Sales Tax Payable	Accounts Receivable		0.00
Invoice	02/22/2015	6	Gonzalez, Adrian	Accounts Receivable	-SPLIT-	35.00	
Invoice	02/22/2015	6	Gonzalez, Adrian	Gym Revenues	Accounts Receivable		35.00
Invoice	02/22/2015	6	Gonzalez, Adrian	Sales Tax Payable	Accounts Receivable		0.00
Invoice	02/22/2015	7	Steele, Lucy	Accounts Receivable	-SPLIT-	35.00	
Invoice	02/22/2015	7	Steele, Lucy	Gym Revenues	Accounts Receivable		35.00
Invoice	02/22/2015	7	Steele, Lucy	Sales Tax Payable	Accounts Receivable		0.00
Invoice	02/22/2015	8	Barnes, Tim	Accounts Receivable	-SPLIT-	35.00	
Invoice	02/22/2015	8	Barnes, Tim	Gym Revenues	Accounts Receivable		35.00
Invoice	02/22/2015	8	Barnes, Tim	Sales Tax Payable	Accounts Receivable		0.00
Invoice	02/22/2015	9	Markum, Robert	Accounts Receivable	-SPLIT-	35.00	
Invoice	02/22/2015	9	Markum, Robert	Gym Revenues	Accounts Receivable		35.00
Invoice	02/22/2015	9	Markum, Robert	Sales Tax Payable	Accounts Receivable		0.00
Invoice	02/22/2015	10	Blackburn, Cindy	Accounts Receivable	-SPLIT-	35.00	
Invoice	02/22/2015	10	Blackburn, Cindy	Gym Revenues	Accounts Receivable		35.00
Invoice	02/22/2015	10	Blackburn, Cindy	Sales Tax Payable	Accounts Receivable		0.00
Invoice	02/22/2015	11	Kline, Jerry	Accounts Receivable	-SPLIT-	35.00	
Invoice	02/22/2015	11	Kline, Jerry	Gym Revenues	Accounts Receivable		35.00
Invoice	02/22/2015	11	Kline, Jerry	Sales Tax Payable	Accounts Receivable		0.00
Sales Receipt	02/23/2015	20	Sampson, Lynn	Undeposited Funds	-SPLIT-	90.00	
Sales Receipt	02/23/2015	20	Sampson, Lynn	Gym Revenues	Undeposited Funds		90.00
Sales Receipt	02/23/2015	20	Sampson, Lynn	Sales Tax Payable	Undeposited Funds		0.00
Bill Pmt - Check	02/25/2015	1017	Swisher Marketing, LLC	Hometown Bank	-SPLIT-		735.00
Bill Pmt - Check	02/25/2015	1017	Swisher Marketing, LLC	Accounts Payable	Hometown Bank	735.00	
Discount	02/25/2015	1017	Swisher Marketing, LLC	Accounts Payable	Hometown Bank	15.00	
Bill Pmt - Check	02/25/2015	1017	Swisher Marketing, LLC	Discounts Earned	Hometown Bank		15.00
Sales Receipt	02/26/2015	21	Gonzalez, Adrian	Undeposited Funds	-SPLIT-	70.00	
Sales Receipt	02/26/2015	21	Gonzalez, Adrian	Gym Revenues	Undeposited Funds		70.00
Sales Receipt	02/26/2015	21	Gonzalez, Adrian	Sales Tax Payable	Undeposited Funds		0.00
Credit Card Charge	02/28/2015		Office Depot	Visa	Office Supplies		56.70
Credit Card Charge	02/28/2015		Office Depot	Office Supplies	Visa	56.70	
Bill Pmt - Check	02/28/2015	1018	City of Springfield	Hometown Bank	Accounts Payable		51.45
Bill Pmt - Check	02/28/2015	1018	City of Springfield	Accounts Payable	Hometown Bank	51.45	
Bill Pmt - Check	02/28/2015	1019	Fit Foods, Inc.	Hometown Bank	Accounts Payable		126.48
Bill Pmt - Check	02/28/2015	1019	Fit Foods, Inc.	Accounts Payable	Hometown Bank	126.48	
Bill Pmt -	02/28/2015	1020	Metro Electric	Hometown Bank	Accounts Payable		183.86

QUICKBOOKS PRACTICE SET

Type	Date	Num	Name	Account	Split	Debit	Credit
Check							
Bill Pmt - Check	02/28/2015	1020	Metro Electric	Accounts Payable	Hometown Bank	183.86	
Bill Pmt - Check	02/28/2015	1021	Time Warner	Hometown Bank	Accounts Payable		147.62
Bill Pmt - Check	02/28/2015	1021	Time Warner	Accounts Payable	Hometown Bank	147.62	
Bill Pmt - Check	02/28/2015	1022	Waste Management	Hometown Bank	Accounts Payable		45.00
Bill Pmt - Check	02/28/2015	1022	Waste Management	Accounts Payable	Hometown Bank	45.00	
Bill	02/28/2015		Metro Electric	Accounts Payable	Electricity		178.86
Bill	02/28/2015		Metro Electric	Electricity	Accounts Payable	178.86	
Bill	02/28/2015		Time Warner	Accounts Payable	Phone / Internet		147.62
Bill	02/28/2015		Time Warner	Phone / Internet	Accounts Payable	147.62	
Bill	02/28/2015		City of Springfield	Accounts Payable	Water		86.45
Bill	02/28/2015		City of Springfield	Water	Accounts Payable	86.45	
Bill	02/28/2015		Waste Management	Accounts Payable	Trash Removal		45.00
Bill	02/28/2015		Waste Management	Trash Removal	Accounts Payable	45.00	
Sales Receipt	02/28/2015	22	Weekly Sales	Undeposited Funds	-SPLIT-	68.85	
Sales Receipt	02/28/2015	22	Weekly Sales	Merchandise Sales	Undeposited Funds		7.50
Sales Receipt	02/28/2015	22	Weekly Sales	Inventory Asset	Undeposited Funds		0.85
Sales Receipt	02/28/2015	22	Weekly Sales	Cost of Goods Sold	Undeposited Funds	0.85	
Sales Receipt	02/28/2015	22	Weekly Sales	Merchandise Sales	Undeposited Funds		8.00
Sales Receipt	02/28/2015	22	Weekly Sales	Inventory Asset	Undeposited Funds		1.48
Sales Receipt	02/28/2015	22	Weekly Sales	Cost of Goods Sold	Undeposited Funds	1.48	
Sales Receipt	02/28/2015	22	Weekly Sales	Merchandise Sales	Undeposited Funds		4.00
Sales Receipt	02/28/2015	22	Weekly Sales	Inventory Asset	Undeposited Funds		0.74
Sales Receipt	02/28/2015	22	Weekly Sales	Cost of Goods Sold	Undeposited Funds	0.74	
Sales Receipt	02/28/2015	22	Weekly Sales	Merchandise Sales	Undeposited Funds		6.00
Sales Receipt	02/28/2015	22	Weekly Sales	Inventory Asset	Undeposited Funds		1.11
Sales Receipt	02/28/2015	22	Weekly Sales	Cost of Goods Sold	Undeposited Funds	1.11	
Sales Receipt	02/28/2015	22	Weekly Sales	Merchandise Sales	Undeposited Funds		18.75
Sales Receipt	02/28/2015	22	Weekly Sales	Inventory Asset	Undeposited Funds		5.25
Sales Receipt	02/28/2015	22	Weekly Sales	Cost of Goods Sold	Undeposited Funds	5.25	
Sales Receipt	02/28/2015	22	Weekly Sales	Merchandise Sales	Undeposited Funds		6.50
Sales Receipt	02/28/2015	22	Weekly Sales	Inventory Asset	Undeposited Funds		0.90
Sales Receipt	02/28/2015	22	Weekly Sales	Cost of Goods Sold	Undeposited Funds	0.90	
Sales Receipt	02/28/2015	22	Weekly Sales	Merchandise Sales	Undeposited Funds		9.75
Sales Receipt	02/28/2015	22	Weekly Sales	Inventory Asset	Undeposited Funds		1.35
Sales Receipt	02/28/2015	22	Weekly Sales	Cost of Goods Sold	Undeposited Funds	1.35	
Sales Receipt	02/28/2015	22	Weekly Sales	Merchandise Sales	Undeposited Funds		3.25
Sales Receipt	02/28/2015	22	Weekly Sales	Inventory Asset	Undeposited Funds		0.45

Sales Receipt	02/28/2015	22	Weekly Sales	Cost of Goods Sold	Undeposited Funds	0.45	
Sales Receipt	02/28/2015	22	Iowa Department of Revenue	Sales Tax Payable	Undeposited Funds		5.10
Deposit	02/28/2015			Hometown Bank	-SPLIT-	228.85	
Deposit	02/28/2015		Sampson, Lynn	Undeposited Funds	Hometown Bank		90.00
Deposit	02/28/2015		Gonzalez, Adrian	Undeposited Funds	Hometown Bank		70.00
Deposit	02/28/2015		Weekly Sales	Undeposited Funds	Hometown Bank		68.85

5 ENTERING TRANSACTIONS – MARCH

Notes for entering transactions:

- Use Accounts Payable (i.e. Enter Bills and Pay Bills) for monthly expenses and bills (when transactions say Received Bill and Pay Bills).

- Enter Checks as indicated for purchases from local retailers and others.

- Use a Sales Receipt for initial registration fees and membership dues received. Subsequent membership dues will be entered as an Invoice and then Receive Payment.

- Enter Sales Receipts for classes and personal training sessions.

- The default in QuickBooks should be for payments received to go to Undeposited Funds -- you will be told when to Record Deposits.

- Do not worry about depreciation on fixed assets. We assumed the accountant or tax professional maintains details of fixed assets and depreciation.

March Transactions

1. Mar 1: Jules Silverstein paid $90 for a quarterly gym membership.

2. Mar 1: Sold 1 hour of personal training to Lynn Sampson for $35.

3. Mar 2: Received bill from Cool T-shirts Co. in the amount of $45.00 for custom staff t-shirts (uniforms), with terms of 2/10, n/30.

4. Mar 3: Sold 1 hour of personal training to Jim Dean for $35.

5. Mar 3: Allison Hoch paid $90 for a quarterly gym membership.

6. Mar 3: Katie Layton paid $25 for a first time gym registration fee and a monthly membership fee of $35.

7. Mar 4: Received payment of $35 from Lucy Steele for March gym membership.

8. Mar 4: Recorded inventory adjustment: Fitness Haven, LLC gave out 1 free water or sports drink to the first 10 customers. Gave out 4 bottled waters, 3 lemon sports drinks, 1 blue sports drink, and 2 red sports drinks (advertising and promotion). (Total Value of Adjustment - $2.90)

9. Mar 4: Hugo Reyson paid $90 for a quarterly gym membership.

10. Mar 6: Check #1024 to Copper Property Management Co. in the amount of $1,500.00 for March rent.

11. Mar 7: The following table lists the members who signed up and paid (Sales Receipts) for March fitness classes. All classes are $50.

Basic Fitness 101	**Wicked Weights**	**Kardio Killers**	**Yoga Fitness**
Allison Hoch	John Brown	Jerry Kline	Cindy Blackburn
Austin Gates	Daniel Brown	Adrian Gonzalez	Jules Silverstein
Jim Dean	Tim Barnes	Lucy Steele	

12. Mar 7: Total food sales from the week are shown in the table below.

Item	Quantity Sold	Sales Price	Totals
Bottled Water	7	$1.50	$10.50
Sports Drink:			
Lemon		2.00	
Orange	4	2.00	8.00
Blue	2	2.00	4.00
Red	3	2.00	6.00
Energy Drink:			
Regular		3.75	
Sugar-Free	4	3.75	15.00
Nutrition Bar:			
Chocolate	5	3.25	16.25
Vanilla		3.25	
Peanut Butter	3	3.25	9.75
Subtotal			**69.50**
Sales Tax			**5.56**
Total			**75.06**

13. Mar 7: Deposited all Undeposited funds from the first week of the month into the checking account for a total of $1,060.06.

14. Mar 8: Richard Halpert paid $90 for a quarterly gym membership.

15. Mar 9: Check #1025 to Cody's Cleaning Co. in the amount of $250.00 for a complete gym cleaning (Janitorial Expense).

16. Mar 9: Pay Sales Taxes for sales taxes due through February 28 with check dated Mar. 9, starting check #1026 in the amount of $11.44.

   Note: Make sure to use the Pay Sales Tax feature and do not just write a check.

17. Mar 10: John Lockhart paid $25 for a first time gym registration fee and a monthly membership fee of $35.

18. Mar 10: Received payment of $35 from Robert Markum for March gym membership.

19. Mar 11: Paid bill from Cool T-shirts Co. (minus 2% discount) with check #1027 in the amount of $44.10.

20. Mar 11: Purchase order #2 to Fit Foods, Inc. in the amount of $91.86 to purchase the following inventory items:

Item	Quantity	Unit Cost	Total Cost	Sales Price
Bottled Water	48	$0.17	$8.16	$1.50
Sports Drink:				
Lemon	12	0.37	4.44	2.00
Orange	24	0.37	8.88	2.00
Blue	48	0.37	17.76	2.00
Red	6	0.37	2.22	2.00
Energy Drink:				
Regular	24	1.05	25.20	3.75
Sugar-Free	6	1.05	6.30	3.75
Nutrition Bar:				
Chocolate	24	0.45	10.80	3.25
Vanilla	12	0.45	5.40	3.25
Peanut Butter	6	0.45	2.70	3.25

21. Mar 11: Jack Sheppert paid $90 for a quarterly gym membership.

22. Mar 12: Received payment of $35 each from Daniel Brown and Adrian Gonzalez for March gym membership.

23. Mar 13: Kate Austino paid $25 for a first time gym registration fee and a monthly membership fee of $35.

24. Mar 14: Total food sales from the week are shown in the table below:

Item	Quantity Sold	Sales Price	Totals
Bottled Water	3	$1.50	$4.50
Sports Drink:			
Lemon	2	2.00	4.00
Orange		2.00	
Blue	1	2.00	2.00
Red	2	2.00	4.00
Energy Drink:			
Regular		3.75	
Sugar-Free	2	3.75	7.50
Nutrition Bar:			
Chocolate	1	3.25	3.25
Vanilla	1	3.25	3.25
Peanut Butter		3.25	
Subtotal			**28.50**
Sales Tax			**2.28**
Total			**30.78**

25. Mar 14: Deposited all Undeposited funds from the second week of the month into the checking account for a total of $435.78.

26. Mar 16: Received payment of $35 from Cindy Blackburn for March gym membership.

27. Mar 17: Sold 1 hour of personal training to Cindy Blackburn and Jim Dean for $35 each.

28. Mar 18: Jim Sawyer paid $25 for a first time gym registration fee and a monthly membership fee of $35.

29. Mar 19: Christian Sheppert paid $90 for a quarterly gym membership.

30. Mar 20: Sold 1 hour of personal training to Kate Austino for $35.

31. Mar 20: Received payment of $35 each from Jerry Kline and Tim Barnes for March gym membership.

32. Mar 21: Danielle Russell paid $25 for a first time gym registration fee and a monthly membership fee of $35.

33. Mar 21: Total food sales from the week are shown below:

Item	Quantity Sold	Sales Price	Totals
Bottled Water	5	$1.50	7.50
Sports Drink:			
Lemon		2.00	
Orange	2	2.00	4.00
Blue	3	2.00	6.00
Red	1	2.00	2.00
Energy Drink:			
Regular	3	3.75	
Sugar-Free		3.75	11.25
Nutrition Bar:			
Chocolate	3	3.25	9.75
Vanilla	1	3.25	3.25
Peanut Butter	2	3.25	6.50
Subtotal			**50.25**
Sales Tax			**4.02**
Total			**54.27**

34. Mar 21: Deposited all Undeposited funds from the third week of the month into the checking account for a total of $474.27.

35. Mar 22: Received partial inventory and the bill from purchase order #2 from Fit Foods, Inc. Red sports drink was not available because it was discontinued and Fit Foods, Inc. was out of stock of vanilla nutrition bars. The new amount due is $84.24. The terms are n/30.

36. Mar 24: Benny Linus paid $25 for a first time gym registration fee and a monthly membership fee of $35.

37. Mar 25: Issued a refund of $35 to Benny Linus who canceled his membership because he decided working out is too hard. (The refund was for the 1 month membership Benny purchased. The registration fee is non-refundable.) Write check #1028 for the refund.

38. Mar 26: Sent invoices to the following members in the amount of $35 for April membership with terms of n/30:

    - Adrian Gonzalez
    - Lucy Steele
    - Tim Barnes
    - Robert Markum
    - Katie Layton
    - John Lockhart
    - Kate Austino
    - Jim Sawyer

    Note: Jerry Kline, Daniel Brown, Cindy Blackburn, and Danielle Russell decided not to renew their membership.

39. Mar 27: Check #1029 to Rob's Repairs in the amount of $220.00 for repairing 2 broken machines.

40. Mar 28: Sold 2 hours of personal training to Adrian Gonzalez for a total of $70.

41. Mar 30: Paid all bills (regardless of the due date) for a total of $542.17 (assign check numbers 1030 to 1034).

42. Mar 31: Received bill from Time Warner in the amount of $147.62 for phone, internet, and cable services with terms of n/30.

43. Mar 31: Received bill from Metro Electric Co. in the amount of $128.86 for electricity with terms of n/30.

44. Mar 31: Received bill from City of Springfield in the amount of for $79.45 for water with terms of n/30.

45. Mar 31: Received bill from Waste Management in the amount of $45.00 for trash removal with terms of n/30.

46. Mar 31: Total food sales from the week are shown in the table below:

Item	Quantity Sold	Sales Price	Totals
Bottled Water	10	$1.50	15.00
Sports Drink:			
Lemon	3	2.00	6.00
Orange	3	2.00	6.00
Blue	5	2.00	10.00
Red		2.00	
Energy Drink:			
Regular	5	3.75	18.75
Sugar-Free	2	3.75	7.50
Nutrition Bar:			
Chocolate	2	3.25	6.50
Vanilla	2	3.25	6.50
Peanut Butter	4	3.25	13.00
Subtotal			**89.25**
Sales Tax			**7.14**
Total			**96.39**

47. Mar 31: Deposited all Undeposited funds into the checking account for a total of $226.39.

Reconcile Accounts

Use the following information to reconcile the checking account:

Bank Statement Ending Date	3/31/2015
Bank Statement Ending Balance	$117,344.38
Outstanding Checks: Check # 1029 $220.00 Check # 1030 $86.45 Check # 1032 $178.86 Check # 1033 $147.62 Check # 1034 $45.00	Outstanding Deposits: 3/31/2015 $226.39

Use the following information to reconcile the Visa credit card account:

Bank Statement Ending Date	3/31/2015
Bank Statement Ending Balance	$56.70
Outstanding Items: None	

After reconciling the credit card account, select to write a check for payment now. Enter the payment date of Apr. 1, payable to Great American Bank with check number 1035.

QUICKBOOKS PRACTICE SET

Check Your Results

Create the following reports and compare them to the following reports. (Make sure to set the dates for March)

Balance Sheet

	Mar 31, 13
ASSETS	
Current Assets	
Checking/Savings	
Checking - Hometown Bank	116,892.84
Total Checking/Savings	116,892.84
Accounts Receivable	
Accounts Receivable	280.00
Total Accounts Receivable	280.00
Other Current Assets	
Inventory Asset	131.16
Total Other Current Assets	131.16
Total Current Assets	117,304.00
Fixed Assets	
Office Furniture and Equipment	4,123.15
Furniture and Equipment	81,200.00
Leasehold Improvements	52,736.89
Total Fixed Assets	138,060.04
Other Assets	
Security Deposits Assets	3,000.00
Total Other Assets	3,000.00
TOTAL ASSETS	258,364.04
LIABILITIES & EQUITY	
Liabilities	
Current Liabilities	
Accounts Payable	
Accounts Payable	400.93

Total Accounts Payable	400.93
Credit Cards	
Visa	56.70
Total Credit Cards	56.70
Other Current Liabilities	
Sales Tax Payable	19.00
Total Other Current Liabilities	19.00
Total Current Liabilities	476.63
Long Term Liabilities	
Note Payable - Hometown Bank	250,000.00
Total Long Term Liabilities	250,000.00
Total Liabilities	250,476.63
Equity	
Tom Martin	
Tom - Owner's Contribution	5,000.00
Total Tom Martin	5,000.00
Joe Watson	
Joe - Owner's Contributions	5,000.00
Total Joe Watson	5,000.00
Nancy Clemens	
Nancy - Owner's Contributions	5,000.00
Total Nancy Clemens	5,000.00
Net Income	-7,112.59
Total Equity	7,887.41
TOTAL LIABILITIES & EQUITY	**258,364.04**

Profit & Loss

	Jan 13	Feb 13	Mar 13	TOTAL
Ordinary Income/Expense				
Income				
Discounts Earned	0.00	19.70	0.90	20.60
Gym Fees	0.00	1,235.00	1,790.00	3,025.00
Merchandise Sales	0.00	143.00	237.50	380.50
Registration Fees	0.00	175.00	150.00	325.00
Total Income	0.00	1,572.70	2,178.40	3,751.10
Cost of Goods Sold				
Cost of Goods Sold	0.00	27.04	43.32	70.36
Total COGS	0.00	27.04	43.32	70.36
Gross Profit	0.00	1,545.66	2,135.08	3,680.74
Expense				
Cleaning Supplies	0.00	68.97	0.00	68.97
Damaged Inventory	0.00	6.30	0.00	6.30
Fitness Supplies	0.00	235.00	0.00	235.00
Advertising and Promotion	225.00	900.00	2.90	1,127.90
Computer and Internet Expenses	550.00	0.00	0.00	550.00
Janitorial Expense	0.00	0.00	250.00	250.00
Office Supplies	136.67	56.70	0.00	193.37
Professional Fees				
Accounting Fees	0.00	450.00	0.00	450.00
Legal Fees	1,785.00	0.00	0.00	1,785.00
Total Professional Fees	1,785.00	450.00	0.00	2,235.00
Rent Expense	1,500.00	1,500.00	1,500.00	4,500.00
Repairs and Maintenance	0.00	75.00	220.00	295.00
Uniforms	0.00	0.00	45.00	45.00
Utilities				
Trash Removal	45.00	45.00	45.00	135.00
Water	51.45	86.45	79.45	217.35
Electricity	183.86	178.86	128.86	491.58
Phone and Internet	147.62	147.62	147.62	442.86
Total Utilities	427.93	457.93	400.93	1,286.79
Total Expense	4,624.60	3,749.90	2,418.83	10,793.33
Net Ordinary Income	-4,624.60	-2,204.24	-283.75	-7,112.59
Net Income	**-4,624.60**	**-2,204.24**	**-283.75**	**-7,112.59**

Accounts Receivable Aging Detail

	Type	Date	Num	Name	Terms	Due Date	Open Balance
Current							
	Invoice	03/26/2015	13	Gonzalez, Adrian	Net 30	04/25/2015	35.00
	Invoice	03/26/2015	14	Steele, Lucy	Net 30	04/25/2015	35.00
	Invoice	03/26/2015	15	Barnes, Tim	Net 30	04/25/2015	35.00
	Invoice	03/26/2015	16	Markum, Robert	Net 30	04/25/2015	35.00
	Invoice	03/26/2015	17	Layton, Katie	Net 30	04/25/2015	35.00
	Invoice	03/26/2015	18	Lockhart, John	Net 30	04/25/2015	35.00
	Invoice	03/26/2015	19	Austino, Kate	Net 30	04/25/2015	35.00
	Invoice	03/26/2015	20	Sawyer, Jim	Net 30	04/25/2015	35.00
Total Current							280.00

Accounts Payable Aging Detail

	Type	Date	Name	Due Date	Open Balance
Current					
	Bill	03/31/2015	Waste Management	04/10/2015	45.00
	Bill	03/31/2015	Time Warner	04/30/2015	147.62
	Bill	03/31/2015	Metro Electric Co.	04/30/2015	128.86
	Bill	03/31/2015	City of Springfield	04/30/2015	79.45
Total Current					400.93

Open Purchase Orders Detail

	Date	Name	Qty	Rcv'd	Backordered	Amount	Open Balance
Inventory							
Nutrition Bar							
Vanilla Bar							
	03/11/2015	Fit Foods, Inc.	12.00	0.00	12.00	5.40	5.40
Total Vanilla Bar			12.00	0.00	12.00	5.40	5.40
Total Nutrition Bar			12.00	0.00	12.00	5.40	5.40
Sports Drink							
Red							
	03/11/2015	Fit Foods, Inc.	6.00	0.00	6.00	2.22	2.22
Total Red			6.00	0.00	6.00	2.22	2.22
Total Sports Drink			6.00	0.00	6.00	2.22	2.22
Total Inventory			18.00	0.00	18.00	7.62	7.62
TOTAL			18.00	0.00	18.00	7.62	7.62

Sales by Customer Detail

	Type	Date	Num	Item	Qty	Sales Price	Amount
Austino, Kate							
	Sales Receipt	03/13/2015	44	Registration Fee	1.00	25.00	25.00
	Sales Receipt	03/13/2015	44	Monthly membership	1.00	35.00	35.00
	Sales Receipt	03/20/2015	50	Personal Training (Personal Training)	1.00	35.00	35.00
	Invoice	03/26/2015	19	Monthly membership	1.00	35.00	35.00
Total Austino, Kate					4.00		130.00
Barnes, Tim							
	Sales Receipt	03/07/2015	34	Wicked Weights	1.00	50.00	50.00
	Invoice	03/26/2015	15	Monthly membership	1.00	35.00	35.00
Total Barnes, Tim					2.00		85.00
Blackburn, Cindy							
	Sales Receipt	03/07/2015	38	Yoga Fitness	1.00	50.00	50.00
	Sales Receipt	03/17/2015	46	Personal Training (Personal Training)	1.00	35.00	35.00
Total Blackburn, Cindy					2.00		85.00
Brown, Daniel							
	Sales Receipt	03/07/2015	33	Wicked Weights	1.00	50.00	50.00
Total Brown, Daniel					1.00		50.00
brown, John							
	Sales Receipt	03/07/2015	32	Wicked Weights	1.00	50.00	50.00
Total brown, John					1.00		50.00
Dean, Jim							
	Sales Receipt	03/03/2015	25	Personal Training (Personal Training)	1.00	35.00	35.00
	Sales Receipt	03/07/2015	31	Basic Fitness 101	1.00	50.00	50.00
	Sales Receipt	03/17/2015	47	Personal Training (Personal Training)	1.00	35.00	35.00
Total Dean, Jim					3.00		120.00
Gates, Austin							
	Sales Receipt	03/07/2015	30	Basic Fitness 101	1.00	50.00	50.00
Total Gates, Austin					1.00		50.00
Gonzalez, Adrian							
	Sales Receipt	03/07/2015	36	Kardio Killers	1.00	50.00	50.00

QUICKBOOKS PRACTICE SET

	Invoice	03/26/2015	13	Monthly membership	1.00	35.00	35.00
	Sales Receipt	03/28/2015	54	Personal Training (Personal Training)	2.00	35.00	70.00
Total Gonzalez, Adrian					4.00		155.00
Halpert, Richard							
	Sales Receipt	03/08/2015	41	Quarterly memberships	1.00	90.00	90.00
Total Halpert, Richard					1.00		90.00
Hoch, Allison							
	Sales Receipt	03/03/2015	26	Quarterly memberships	1.00	90.00	90.00
	Sales Receipt	03/07/2015	29	Basic Fitness 101	1.00	50.00	50.00
Total Hoch, Allison					2.00		140.00
Kline, Jerry							
	Sales Receipt	03/07/2015	35	Kardio Killers	1.00	50.00	50.00
Total Kline, Jerry					1.00		50.00
Layton, Katie							
	Sales Receipt	03/03/2015	27	Registration Fee	1.00	25.00	25.00
	Sales Receipt	03/03/2015	27	Monthly membership	1.00	35.00	35.00
	Invoice	03/26/2015	17	Monthly membership	1.00	35.00	35.00
Total Layton, Katie					3.00		95.00
Linus, Benny							
	Sales Receipt	03/24/2015	53	Registration Fee	1.00	25.00	25.00
	Sales Receipt	03/24/2015	53	Monthly membership	1.00	35.00	35.00
	Credit Memo	03/25/2015	12	Monthly membership	-1.00	35.00	-35.00
Total Linus, Benny					1.00		25.00
Lockhart, John							
	Sales Receipt	03/10/2015	42	Registration Fee	1.00	25.00	25.00
	Sales Receipt	03/10/2015	42	Monthly membership	1.00	35.00	35.00
	Invoice	03/26/2015	18	Monthly membership	1.00	35.00	35.00
Total Lockhart, John					3.00		95.00
Markum, Robert							
	Invoice	03/26/2015	16	Monthly membership	1.00	35.00	35.00
Total Markum, Robert					1.00		35.00
Reyson, Hugo							
	Sales	03/04/2015	28	Quarterly memberships	1.00	90.00	90.00

		Receipt				1.00	90.00
Total Reyson, Hugo						1.00	90.00
Russell, Danielle							
		Sales Receipt	03/21/2015	51	Registration Fee	1.00	25.00	25.00
		Sales Receipt	03/21/2015	51	Monthly membership	1.00	35.00	35.00
Total Russell, Danielle						2.00	60.00
Sampson, Lynn							
		Sales Receipt	03/01/2015	24	Personal Training (Personal Training)	1.00	35.00	35.00
Total Sampson, Lynn						1.00	35.00
Sawyer, Jim							
		Sales Receipt	03/18/2015	48	Registration Fee	1.00	25.00	25.00
		Sales Receipt	03/18/2015	48	Monthly membership	1.00	35.00	35.00
		Invoice	03/26/2015	20	Monthly membership	1.00	35.00	35.00
Total Sawyer, Jim						3.00	95.00
Sheppert, Christian							
		Sales Receipt	03/19/2015	49	Quarterly memberships	1.00	90.00	90.00
Total Sheppert, Christian						1.00	90.00
Sheppert, Jack							
		Sales Receipt	03/11/2015	43	Quarterly memberships	1.00	90.00	90.00
Total Sheppert, Jack						1.00	90.00
Silverstein, Jules							
		Sales Receipt	03/01/2015	23	Quarterly memberships	1.00	90.00	90.00
		Sales Receipt	03/07/2015	39	Yoga Fitness	1.00	50.00	50.00
Total Silverstein, Jules						2.00	140.00
Steele, Lucy							
		Sales Receipt	03/07/2015	37	Kardio Killers	1.00	50.00	50.00
		Invoice	03/26/2015	14	Monthly membership	1.00	35.00	35.00
Total Steele, Lucy						2.00	85.00
Weekly Sales							
		Sales Receipt	03/07/2015	40	Bottled Water	7.00	1.50	10.50
		Sales Receipt	03/07/2015	40	Sports Drink:Orange	4.00	2.00	8.00
		Sales Receipt	03/07/2015	40	Sports Drink:Blue	2.00	2.00	4.00

QUICKBOOKS PRACTICE SET

	Sales Receipt	03/07/2015	40	Sports Drink:Red	3.00	2.00	6.00
	Sales Receipt	03/07/2015	40	Energy Drink:Sugar-Free	4.00	3.75	15.00
	Sales Receipt	03/07/2015	40	Nutrition Bar:Chocolate	5.00	3.25	16.25
	Sales Receipt	03/07/2015	40	Nutrition Bar:Peanut Butter	3.00	3.25	9.75
	Sales Receipt	03/14/2015	45	Bottled Water	3.00	1.50	4.50
	Sales Receipt	03/14/2015	45	Sports Drink:Lemon	2.00	2.00	4.00
	Sales Receipt	03/14/2015	45	Sports Drink:Blue	1.00	2.00	2.00
	Sales Receipt	03/14/2015	45	Sports Drink:Red	2.00	2.00	4.00
	Sales Receipt	03/14/2015	45	Energy Drink:Sugar-Free	2.00	3.75	7.50
	Sales Receipt	03/14/2015	45	Nutrition Bar:Chocolate	1.00	3.25	3.25
	Sales Receipt	03/14/2015	45	Nutrition Bar:Vanilla	1.00	3.25	3.25
	Sales Receipt	03/21/2015	52	Bottled Water	5.00	1.50	7.50
	Sales Receipt	03/21/2015	52	Sports Drink:Orange	2.00	2.00	4.00
	Sales Receipt	03/21/2015	52	Sports Drink:Blue	3.00	2.00	6.00
	Sales Receipt	03/21/2015	52	Sports Drink:Red	1.00	2.00	2.00
	Sales Receipt	03/21/2015	52	Energy Drink:Regular	3.00	3.75	11.25
	Sales Receipt	03/21/2015	52	Nutrition Bar:Chocolate	3.00	3.25	9.75
	Sales Receipt	03/21/2015	52	Nutrition Bar:Vanilla	1.00	3.25	3.25
	Sales Receipt	03/21/2015	52	Nutrition Bar:Peanut Butter	2.00	3.25	6.50
	Sales Receipt	03/31/2015	55	Bottled Water	10.00	1.50	15.00
	Sales Receipt	03/31/2015	55	Sports Drink:Lemon	3.00	2.00	6.00
	Sales Receipt	03/31/2015	55	Sports Drink:Orange	3.00	2.00	6.00
	Sales Receipt	03/31/2015	55	Sports Drink:Blue	5.00	2.00	10.00
	Sales Receipt	03/31/2015	55	Energy Drink:Regular	5.00	3.75	18.75
	Sales Receipt	03/31/2015	55	Energy Drink:Sugar-Free	2.00	3.75	7.50
	Sales Receipt	03/31/2015	55	Nutrition Bar:Chocolate	2.00	3.25	6.50
	Sales Receipt	03/31/2015	55	Nutrition Bar:Vanilla	2.00	3.25	6.50
	Sales Receipt	03/31/2015	55	Nutrition Bar:Peanut Butter	4.00	3.25	13.00
Total Weekly Sales					96.00		237.50
					139.00		2,177.50

Sales by Item Detail

	Type	Date	Num	Qty	Sales Price	Amount
Inventory						
Bottled Water						
	Sales Receipt	03/07/2015	40	7.00	1.50	10.50
	Sales Receipt	03/14/2015	45	3.00	1.50	4.50
	Sales Receipt	03/21/2015	52	5.00	1.50	7.50
	Sales Receipt	03/31/2015	55	10.00	1.50	15.00
Total Bottled Water				25.00		37.50
Energy Drink						
Regular						
	Sales Receipt	03/21/2015	52	3.00	3.75	11.25
	Sales Receipt	03/31/2015	55	5.00	3.75	18.75
Total Regular				8.00		30.00
Sugar-Free						
	Sales Receipt	03/07/2015	40	4.00	3.75	15.00
	Sales Receipt	03/14/2015	45	2.00	3.75	7.50
	Sales Receipt	03/31/2015	55	2.00	3.75	7.50
Total Sugar-Free				8.00		30.00
Total Energy Drink				16.00		60.00
Nutrition Bar						
Chocolate						
	Sales Receipt	03/07/2015	40	5.00	3.25	16.25
	Sales Receipt	03/14/2015	45	1.00	3.25	3.25
	Sales Receipt	03/21/2015	52	3.00	3.25	9.75
	Sales Receipt	03/31/2015	55	2.00	3.25	6.50
Total Chocolate				11.00		35.75
Peanut Butter						
	Sales Receipt	03/07/2015	40	3.00	3.25	9.75
	Sales Receipt	03/21/2015	52	2.00	3.25	6.50
	Sales Receipt	03/31/2015	55	4.00	3.25	13.00
Total Peanut Butter				9.00		29.25

Vanilla

Sales Receipt	03/14/2015	45	1.00	3.25	3.25
Sales Receipt	03/21/2015	52	1.00	3.25	3.25
Sales Receipt	03/31/2015	55	2.00	3.25	6.50

Total Vanilla   4.00   13.00

Total Nutrition Bar   24.00   78.00

Sports Drink

Blue

Sales Receipt	03/07/2015	40	2.00	2.00	4.00
Sales Receipt	03/14/2015	45	1.00	2.00	2.00
Sales Receipt	03/21/2015	52	3.00	2.00	6.00
Sales Receipt	03/31/2015	55	5.00	2.00	10.00

Total Blue   11.00   22.00

Lemon

Sales Receipt	03/14/2015	45	2.00	2.00	4.00
Sales Receipt	03/31/2015	55	3.00	2.00	6.00

Total Lemon   5.00   10.00

Orange

Sales Receipt	03/07/2015	40	4.00	2.00	8.00
Sales Receipt	03/21/2015	52	2.00	2.00	4.00
Sales Receipt	03/31/2015	55	3.00	2.00	6.00

Total Orange   9.00   18.00

Red

Sales Receipt	03/07/2015	40	3.00	2.00	6.00
Sales Receipt	03/14/2015	45	2.00	2.00	4.00
Sales Receipt	03/21/2015	52	1.00	2.00	2.00

Total Red   6.00   12.00

Total Sports Drink   31.00   62.00

Total Inventory   96.00   237.50

Service

Basic Fitness 101

	Sales Receipt	03/07/2015	29	1.00	50.00	50.00
	Sales Receipt	03/07/2015	30	1.00	50.00	50.00
	Sales Receipt	03/07/2015	31	1.00	50.00	50.00
Total Basic Fitness 101				3.00		150.00

Kardio Killers

	Sales Receipt	03/07/2015	35	1.00	50.00	50.00
	Sales Receipt	03/07/2015	36	1.00	50.00	50.00
	Sales Receipt	03/07/2015	37	1.00	50.00	50.00
Total Kardio Killers				3.00		150.00

Monthly membership

	Sales Receipt	03/03/2015	27	1.00	35.00	35.00
	Sales Receipt	03/10/2015	42	1.00	35.00	35.00
	Sales Receipt	03/13/2015	44	1.00	35.00	35.00
	Sales Receipt	03/18/2015	48	1.00	35.00	35.00
	Sales Receipt	03/21/2015	51	1.00	35.00	35.00
	Sales Receipt	03/24/2015	53	1.00	35.00	35.00
	Credit Memo	03/25/2015	12	-1.00	35.00	-35.00
	Invoice	03/26/2015	13	1.00	35.00	35.00
	Invoice	03/26/2015	14	1.00	35.00	35.00
	Invoice	03/26/2015	15	1.00	35.00	35.00
	Invoice	03/26/2015	16	1.00	35.00	35.00
	Invoice	03/26/2015	17	1.00	35.00	35.00
	Invoice	03/26/2015	18	1.00	35.00	35.00
	Invoice	03/26/2015	19	1.00	35.00	35.00
	Invoice	03/26/2015	20	1.00	35.00	35.00
Total Monthly membership				13.00		455.00

Personal Training (Personal Training)

	Sales Receipt	03/01/2015	24	1.00	35.00	35.00
	Sales Receipt	03/03/2015	25	1.00	35.00	35.00
	Sales Receipt	03/17/2015	46	1.00	35.00	35.00
	Sales Receipt	03/17/2015	47	1.00	35.00	35.00
	Sales Receipt	03/20/2015	50	1.00	35.00	35.00
	Sales Receipt	03/28/2015	54	2.00	35.00	70.00
Total Personal Training (Personal Training)				7.00		245.00

Quarterly memberships

QUICKBOOKS PRACTICE SET

Sales Receipt	03/01/2015	23	1.00	90.00	90.00
Sales Receipt	03/03/2015	26	1.00	90.00	90.00
Sales Receipt	03/04/2015	28	1.00	90.00	90.00
Sales Receipt	03/08/2015	41	1.00	90.00	90.00
Sales Receipt	03/11/2015	43	1.00	90.00	90.00
Sales Receipt	03/19/2015	49	1.00	90.00	90.00

Total Quarterly memberships   6.00   540.00

Registration Fee

Sales Receipt	03/03/2015	27	1.00	25.00	25.00
Sales Receipt	03/10/2015	42	1.00	25.00	25.00
Sales Receipt	03/13/2015	44	1.00	25.00	25.00
Sales Receipt	03/18/2015	48	1.00	25.00	25.00
Sales Receipt	03/21/2015	51	1.00	25.00	25.00
Sales Receipt	03/24/2015	53	1.00	25.00	25.00

Total Registration Fee   6.00   150.00

Wicked Weights

Sales Receipt	03/07/2015	32	1.00	50.00	50.00
Sales Receipt	03/07/2015	33	1.00	50.00	50.00
Sales Receipt	03/07/2015	34	1.00	50.00	50.00

Total Wicked Weights   3.00   150.00

Yoga Fitness

Sales Receipt	03/07/2015	38	1.00	50.00	50.00
Sales Receipt	03/07/2015	39	1.00	50.00	50.00

Total Yoga Fitness   2.00   100.00

Total Service   43.00   1,940.00

                                139.00   2,177.50

Inventory Stock Status by Item

	On Hand	On PO	Next Deliv
Inventory			
Bottled Water	59.00	0.00	
Energy Drink			
Regular	40.00	0.00	
Sugar-Free	6.00	0.00	
Energy Drink - Other	0.00	0.00	
Total Energy Drink	46.00	0.00	
Nutrition Bar			
Chocolate	30.00	0.00	
Peanut Butter	19.00	0.00	
Vanilla	15.00	12.00	03/11/2015
Nutrition Bar - Other	0.00	0.00	
Total Nutrition Bar	64.00	12.00	
Sports Drink			
Blue	49.00	0.00	
Lemon	21.00	0.00	
Orange	34.00	0.00	
Red	15.00	6.00	03/11/2015
Sports Drink - Other	0.00	0.00	
Total Sports Drink	119.00	6.00	

Transaction List by Date

Type	Date	Num	Name	Account	Split	Debit	Credit
Check	03/01/2015	1023	Great American Bank	Hometown Bank	Visa		68.97
Check	03/01/2015	1023	Great American Bank	Visa	Hometown Bank	68.97	
Sales Receipt	03/01/2015	23	Silverstein, Jules	Undeposited Funds	-SPLIT-	90.00	
Sales Receipt	03/01/2015	23	Silverstein, Jules	Gym Revenues	Undeposited Funds		90.00
Sales Receipt	03/01/2015	23	Silverstein, Jules	Sales Tax Payable	Undeposited Funds	0.00	
Sales Receipt	03/01/2015	24	Sampson, Lynn	Undeposited Funds	-SPLIT-	35.00	
Sales Receipt	03/01/2015	24	Sampson, Lynn	Gym Revenues	Undeposited Funds		35.00
Sales Receipt	03/01/2015	24	Sampson, Lynn	Sales Tax Payable	Undeposited Funds	0.00	

QUICKBOOKS PRACTICE SET

Type	Date	Num	Name	Account	Split	Debit	Credit
Bill	03/02/2015		Cool T-Shirts Co.	Accounts Payable	Uniforms		45.00
Bill	03/02/2015		Cool T-Shirts Co.	Uniforms	Accounts Payable	45.00	
Bill	03/02/2015		Fit Foods, Inc.	Accounts Payable	-SPLIT-		84.24
Bill	03/02/2015		Fit Foods, Inc.	Inventory Asset	Accounts Payable	8.16	
Bill	03/02/2015		Fit Foods, Inc.	Inventory Asset	Accounts Payable	4.44	
Bill	03/02/2015		Fit Foods, Inc.	Inventory Asset	Accounts Payable	8.88	
Bill	03/02/2015		Fit Foods, Inc.	Inventory Asset	Accounts Payable	17.76	
Bill	03/02/2015		Fit Foods, Inc.	Inventory Asset	Accounts Payable	0.00	
Bill	03/02/2015		Fit Foods, Inc.	Inventory Asset	Accounts Payable	25.20	
Bill	03/02/2015		Fit Foods, Inc.	Inventory Asset	Accounts Payable	6.30	
Bill	03/02/2015		Fit Foods, Inc.	Inventory Asset	Accounts Payable	10.80	
Bill	03/02/2015		Fit Foods, Inc.	Inventory Asset	Accounts Payable	0.00	
Bill	03/02/2015		Fit Foods, Inc.	Inventory Asset	Accounts Payable	2.70	
Sales Receipt	03/03/2015	25	Dean, Jim	Undeposited Funds	-SPLIT-	35.00	
Sales Receipt	03/03/2015	25	Dean, Jim	Gym Revenues	Undeposited Funds		35.00
Sales Receipt	03/03/2015	25	Dean, Jim	Sales Tax Payable	Undeposited Funds		0.00
Sales Receipt	03/03/2015	26	Hoch, Allison	Undeposited Funds	-SPLIT-	90.00	
Sales Receipt	03/03/2015	26	Hoch, Allison	Gym Revenues	Undeposited Funds		90.00
Sales Receipt	03/03/2015	26	Hoch, Allison	Sales Tax Payable	Undeposited Funds		0.00
Sales Receipt	03/03/2015	27	Layton, Katie	Undeposited Funds	-SPLIT-	60.00	
Sales Receipt	03/03/2015	27	Layton, Katie	Registration Fees	Undeposited Funds		25.00
Sales Receipt	03/03/2015	27	Layton, Katie	Gym Revenues	Undeposited Funds		35.00
Sales Receipt	03/03/2015	27	Layton, Katie	Sales Tax Payable	Undeposited Funds		0.00
Payment	03/04/2015		Steele, Lucy	Undeposited Funds	Accounts Receivable	35.00	
Payment	03/04/2015		Steele, Lucy	Accounts Receivable	Undeposited Funds		35.00
Inventory Adjust	03/04/2015	1		Advertising and Promotion	-SPLIT-	2.90	
Inventory Adjust	03/04/2015	1		Inventory Asset	Advertising and Promotion		0.68
Inventory Adjust	03/04/2015	1		Inventory Asset	Advertising and Promotion		1.11
Inventory Adjust	03/04/2015	1		Inventory Asset	Advertising and Promotion		0.37
Inventory Adjust	03/04/2015	1		Inventory Asset	Advertising and Promotion		0.74
Sales Receipt	03/04/2015	28	Reyson, Hugo	Undeposited Funds	-SPLIT-	90.00	
Sales Receipt	03/04/2015	28	Reyson, Hugo	Gym Revenues	Undeposited Funds		90.00
Sales Receipt	03/04/2015	28	Reyson, Hugo	Sales Tax Payable	Undeposited Funds		0.00
Check	03/06/2015	1024	Copper Property Management Co	Hometown Bank	Rent Expense		1,500.00
Check	03/06/2015	1024	Copper Property Management Co	Rent Expense	Hometown Bank	1,500.00	
Sales Receipt	03/07/2015	29	Hoch, Allison	Undeposited Funds	-SPLIT-	50.00	
Sales Receipt	03/07/2015	29	Hoch, Allison	Gym Revenues	Undeposited Funds		50.00

Sales Receipt	03/07/2015	29	Hoch, Allison	Sales Tax Payable	Undeposited Funds	0.00	
Sales Receipt	03/07/2015	30	Gates, Austin	Undeposited Funds	-SPLIT-	50.00	
Sales Receipt	03/07/2015	30	Gates, Austin	Gym Revenues	Undeposited Funds		50.00
Sales Receipt	03/07/2015	30	Gates, Austin	Sales Tax Payable	Undeposited Funds	0.00	
Sales Receipt	03/07/2015	31	Dean, Jim	Undeposited Funds	-SPLIT-	50.00	
Sales Receipt	03/07/2015	31	Dean, Jim	Gym Revenues	Undeposited Funds		50.00
Sales Receipt	03/07/2015	31	Dean, Jim	Sales Tax Payable	Undeposited Funds	0.00	
Sales Receipt	03/07/2015	32	brown, John	Undeposited Funds	-SPLIT-	50.00	
Sales Receipt	03/07/2015	32	brown, John	Gym Revenues	Undeposited Funds		50.00
Sales Receipt	03/07/2015	32	brown, John	Sales Tax Payable	Undeposited Funds	0.00	
Sales Receipt	03/07/2015	33	Brown, Daniel	Undeposited Funds	-SPLIT-	50.00	
Sales Receipt	03/07/2015	33	Brown, Daniel	Gym Revenues	Undeposited Funds		50.00
Sales Receipt	03/07/2015	33	Brown, Daniel	Sales Tax Payable	Undeposited Funds	0.00	
Sales Receipt	03/07/2015	34	Barnes, Tim	Undeposited Funds	-SPLIT-	50.00	
Sales Receipt	03/07/2015	34	Barnes, Tim	Gym Revenues	Undeposited Funds		50.00
Sales Receipt	03/07/2015	34	Barnes, Tim	Sales Tax Payable	Undeposited Funds	0.00	
Sales Receipt	03/07/2015	35	Kline, Jerry	Undeposited Funds	-SPLIT-	50.00	
Sales Receipt	03/07/2015	35	Kline, Jerry	Gym Revenues	Undeposited Funds		50.00
Sales Receipt	03/07/2015	35	Kline, Jerry	Sales Tax Payable	Undeposited Funds	0.00	
Sales Receipt	03/07/2015	36	Gonzalez, Adrian	Undeposited Funds	-SPLIT-	50.00	
Sales Receipt	03/07/2015	36	Gonzalez, Adrian	Gym Revenues	Undeposited Funds		50.00
Sales Receipt	03/07/2015	36	Gonzalez, Adrian	Sales Tax Payable	Undeposited Funds	0.00	
Sales Receipt	03/07/2015	37	Steele, Lucy	Undeposited Funds	-SPLIT-	50.00	
Sales Receipt	03/07/2015	37	Steele, Lucy	Gym Revenues	Undeposited Funds		50.00
Sales Receipt	03/07/2015	37	Steele, Lucy	Sales Tax Payable	Undeposited Funds	0.00	
Sales Receipt	03/07/2015	38	Blackburn, Cindy	Undeposited Funds	-SPLIT-	50.00	
Sales Receipt	03/07/2015	38	Blackburn, Cindy	Gym Revenues	Undeposited Funds		50.00
Sales Receipt	03/07/2015	38	Blackburn, Cindy	Sales Tax Payable	Undeposited Funds	0.00	
Sales Receipt	03/07/2015	39	Silverstein, Jules	Undeposited Funds	-SPLIT-	50.00	
Sales Receipt	03/07/2015	39	Silverstein, Jules	Gym Revenues	Undeposited Funds		50.00
Sales Receipt	03/07/2015	39	Silverstein, Jules	Sales Tax Payable	Undeposited Funds	0.00	
Sales Receipt	03/07/2015	40	Weekly Sales	Undeposited Funds	-SPLIT-	75.06	
Sales Receipt	03/07/2015	40	Weekly Sales	Merchandise Sales	Undeposited Funds		10.50
Sales Receipt	03/07/2015	40	Weekly Sales	Inventory Asset	Undeposited Funds		1.19
Sales Receipt	03/07/2015	40	Weekly Sales	Cost of Goods Sold	Undeposited Funds	1.19	
Sales Receipt	03/07/2015	40	Weekly Sales	Merchandise Sales	Undeposited Funds		8.00
Sales Receipt	03/07/2015	40	Weekly Sales	Inventory Asset	Undeposited Funds		1.48
Sales Receipt	03/07/2015	40	Weekly Sales	Cost of Goods Sold	Undeposited Funds	1.48	

Type	Date	Num	Name	Account	Split	Debit	Credit
Sales Receipt	03/07/2015	40	Weekly Sales	Merchandise Sales	Undeposited Funds		4.00
Sales Receipt	03/07/2015	40	Weekly Sales	Inventory Asset	Undeposited Funds		0.74
Sales Receipt	03/07/2015	40	Weekly Sales	Cost of Goods Sold	Undeposited Funds	0.74	
Sales Receipt	03/07/2015	40	Weekly Sales	Merchandise Sales	Undeposited Funds		6.00
Sales Receipt	03/07/2015	40	Weekly Sales	Inventory Asset	Undeposited Funds		1.11
Sales Receipt	03/07/2015	40	Weekly Sales	Cost of Goods Sold	Undeposited Funds	1.11	
Sales Receipt	03/07/2015	40	Weekly Sales	Merchandise Sales	Undeposited Funds		15.00
Sales Receipt	03/07/2015	40	Weekly Sales	Inventory Asset	Undeposited Funds		4.20
Sales Receipt	03/07/2015	40	Weekly Sales	Cost of Goods Sold	Undeposited Funds	4.20	
Sales Receipt	03/07/2015	40	Weekly Sales	Merchandise Sales	Undeposited Funds		16.25
Sales Receipt	03/07/2015	40	Weekly Sales	Inventory Asset	Undeposited Funds		2.25
Sales Receipt	03/07/2015	40	Weekly Sales	Cost of Goods Sold	Undeposited Funds	2.25	
Sales Receipt	03/07/2015	40	Weekly Sales	Merchandise Sales	Undeposited Funds		9.75
Sales Receipt	03/07/2015	40	Weekly Sales	Inventory Asset	Undeposited Funds		1.35
Sales Receipt	03/07/2015	40	Weekly Sales	Cost of Goods Sold	Undeposited Funds	1.35	
Sales Receipt	03/07/2015	40	Iowa Department of Revenue	Sales Tax Payable	Undeposited Funds		5.56
Deposit	03/07/2015			Hometown Bank	-SPLIT-	1,060.06	
Deposit	03/07/2015		Silverstein, Jules	Undeposited Funds	Hometown Bank		90.00
Deposit	03/07/2015		Sampson, Lynn	Undeposited Funds	Hometown Bank		35.00
Deposit	03/07/2015		Dean, Jim	Undeposited Funds	Hometown Bank		35.00
Deposit	03/07/2015		Hoch, Allison	Undeposited Funds	Hometown Bank		90.00
Deposit	03/07/2015		Layton, Katie	Undeposited Funds	Hometown Bank		60.00
Deposit	03/07/2015		Steele, Lucy	Undeposited Funds	Hometown Bank		35.00
Deposit	03/07/2015		Reyson, Hugo	Undeposited Funds	Hometown Bank		90.00
Deposit	03/07/2015		Hoch, Allison	Undeposited Funds	Hometown Bank		50.00
Deposit	03/07/2015		Gates, Austin	Undeposited Funds	Hometown Bank		50.00
Deposit	03/07/2015		Dean, Jim	Undeposited Funds	Hometown Bank		50.00
Deposit	03/07/2015		brown, John	Undeposited Funds	Hometown Bank		50.00
Deposit	03/07/2015		Brown, Daniel	Undeposited Funds	Hometown Bank		50.00
Deposit	03/07/2015		Barnes, Tim	Undeposited Funds	Hometown Bank		50.00
Deposit	03/07/2015		Kline, Jerry	Undeposited Funds	Hometown Bank		50.00
Deposit	03/07/2015		Gonzalez, Adrian	Undeposited Funds	Hometown Bank		50.00
Deposit	03/07/2015		Steele, Lucy	Undeposited Funds	Hometown Bank		50.00
Deposit	03/07/2015		Blackburn, Cindy	Undeposited Funds	Hometown Bank		50.00
Deposit	03/07/2015		Silverstein, Jules	Undeposited Funds	Hometown Bank		50.00
Deposit	03/07/2015		Weekly Sales	Undeposited Funds	Hometown Bank		75.06

Type	Date	Num	Name	Account	Split	Debit	Credit
Sales Receipt	03/08/2015	41	Halpert, Richard	Undeposited Funds	-SPLIT-	90.00	
Sales Receipt	03/08/2015	41	Halpert, Richard	Gym Revenues	Undeposited Funds		90.00
Sales Receipt	03/08/2015	41	Halpert, Richard	Sales Tax Payable	Undeposited Funds		0.00
Check	03/09/2015	1025	Cody's Cleaning Co.	Hometown Bank	Janitorial Expense		250.00
Check	03/09/2015	1025	Cody's Cleaning Co.	Janitorial Expense	Hometown Bank	250.00	
Sales Tax Payment	03/09/2015	1026	Iowa Department of Revenue	Hometown Bank	Sales Tax Payable		11.44
Sales Tax Payment	03/09/2015	1026	Iowa Department of Revenue	Sales Tax Payable	Hometown Bank	11.44	
Sales Receipt	03/10/2015	42	Lockhart, John	Undeposited Funds	-SPLIT-	60.00	
Sales Receipt	03/10/2015	42	Lockhart, John	Registration Fees	Undeposited Funds		25.00
Sales Receipt	03/10/2015	42	Lockhart, John	Gym Revenues	Undeposited Funds		35.00
Sales Receipt	03/10/2015	42	Lockhart, John	Sales Tax Payable	Undeposited Funds		0.00
Payment	03/10/2015		Markum, Robert	Undeposited Funds	Accounts Receivable	35.00	
Payment	03/10/2015		Markum, Robert	Accounts Receivable	Undeposited Funds		35.00
Bill Pmt - Check	03/11/2015	1027	Cool T-Shirts Co.	Hometown Bank	-SPLIT-		44.10
Bill Pmt - Check	03/11/2015	1027	Cool T-Shirts Co.	Accounts Payable	Hometown Bank	44.10	
Discount	03/11/2015	1027	Cool T-Shirts Co.	Accounts Payable	Hometown Bank	0.90	
Bill Pmt - Check	03/11/2015	1027	Cool T-Shirts Co.	Discounts Earned	Hometown Bank		0.90
Sales Receipt	03/11/2015	43	Sheppert, Jack	Undeposited Funds	-SPLIT-	90.00	
Sales Receipt	03/11/2015	43	Sheppert, Jack	Gym Revenues	Undeposited Funds		90.00
Sales Receipt	03/11/2015	43	Sheppert, Jack	Sales Tax Payable	Undeposited Funds		0.00
Payment	03/12/2015		Brown, Daniel	Undeposited Funds	Accounts Receivable	35.00	
Payment	03/12/2015		Brown, Daniel	Accounts Receivable	Undeposited Funds		35.00
Payment	03/12/2015		Gonzalez, Adrian	Undeposited Funds	Accounts Receivable	35.00	
Payment	03/12/2015		Gonzalez, Adrian	Accounts Receivable	Undeposited Funds		35.00
Sales Receipt	03/13/2015	44	Austino, Kate	Undeposited Funds	-SPLIT-	60.00	
Sales Receipt	03/13/2015	44	Austino, Kate	Registration Fees	Undeposited Funds		25.00
Sales Receipt	03/13/2015	44	Austino, Kate	Gym Revenues	Undeposited Funds		35.00
Sales Receipt	03/13/2015	44	Austino, Kate	Sales Tax Payable	Undeposited Funds		0.00
Sales Receipt	03/14/2015	45	Weekly Sales	Undeposited Funds	-SPLIT-	30.78	
Sales Receipt	03/14/2015	45	Weekly Sales	Merchandise Sales	Undeposited Funds		4.50
Sales Receipt	03/14/2015	45	Weekly Sales	Inventory Asset	Undeposited Funds		0.51
Sales Receipt	03/14/2015	45	Weekly Sales	Cost of Goods Sold	Undeposited Funds	0.51	
Sales Receipt	03/14/2015	45	Weekly Sales	Merchandise Sales	Undeposited Funds		4.00
Sales Receipt	03/14/2015	45	Weekly Sales	Inventory Asset	Undeposited Funds		0.74
Sales Receipt	03/14/2015	45	Weekly Sales	Cost of Goods Sold	Undeposited Funds	0.74	
Sales Receipt	03/14/2015	45	Weekly Sales	Merchandise Sales	Undeposited Funds		2.00
Sales Receipt	03/14/2015	45	Weekly Sales	Inventory Asset	Undeposited Funds		0.37

QUICKBOOKS PRACTICE SET

Sales Receipt	03/14/2015	45	Weekly Sales	Cost of Goods Sold	Undeposited Funds	0.37	
Sales Receipt	03/14/2015	45	Weekly Sales	Merchandise Sales	Undeposited Funds		4.00
Sales Receipt	03/14/2015	45	Weekly Sales	Inventory Asset	Undeposited Funds		0.74
Sales Receipt	03/14/2015	45	Weekly Sales	Cost of Goods Sold	Undeposited Funds	0.74	
Sales Receipt	03/14/2015	45	Weekly Sales	Merchandise Sales	Undeposited Funds		7.50
Sales Receipt	03/14/2015	45	Weekly Sales	Inventory Asset	Undeposited Funds		2.10
Sales Receipt	03/14/2015	45	Weekly Sales	Cost of Goods Sold	Undeposited Funds	2.10	
Sales Receipt	03/14/2015	45	Weekly Sales	Merchandise Sales	Undeposited Funds		3.25
Sales Receipt	03/14/2015	45	Weekly Sales	Inventory Asset	Undeposited Funds		0.45
Sales Receipt	03/14/2015	45	Weekly Sales	Cost of Goods Sold	Undeposited Funds	0.45	
Sales Receipt	03/14/2015	45	Weekly Sales	Merchandise Sales	Undeposited Funds		3.25
Sales Receipt	03/14/2015	45	Weekly Sales	Inventory Asset	Undeposited Funds		0.45
Sales Receipt	03/14/2015	45	Weekly Sales	Cost of Goods Sold	Undeposited Funds	0.45	
Sales Receipt	03/14/2015	45	Iowa Department of Revenue	Sales Tax Payable	Undeposited Funds		2.28
Deposit	03/14/2015			Hometown Bank	-SPLIT-	435.78	
Deposit	03/14/2015		Halpert, Richard	Undeposited Funds	Hometown Bank		90.00
Deposit	03/14/2015		Lockhart, John	Undeposited Funds	Hometown Bank		60.00
Deposit	03/14/2015		Markum, Robert	Undeposited Funds	Hometown Bank		35.00
Deposit	03/14/2015		Sheppert, Jack	Undeposited Funds	Hometown Bank		90.00
Deposit	03/14/2015		Brown, Daniel	Undeposited Funds	Hometown Bank		35.00
Deposit	03/14/2015		Gonzalez, Adrian	Undeposited Funds	Hometown Bank		35.00
Deposit	03/14/2015		Austino, Kate	Undeposited Funds	Hometown Bank		60.00
Deposit	03/14/2015		Weekly Sales	Undeposited Funds	Hometown Bank		30.78
Payment	03/16/2015		Blackburn, Cindy	Undeposited Funds	Accounts Receivable	35.00	
Payment	03/16/2015		Blackburn, Cindy	Accounts Receivable	Undeposited Funds		35.00
Sales Receipt	03/17/2015	46	Blackburn, Cindy	Undeposited Funds	-SPLIT-	35.00	
Sales Receipt	03/17/2015	46	Blackburn, Cindy	Gym Revenues	Undeposited Funds		35.00
Sales Receipt	03/17/2015	46	Blackburn, Cindy	Sales Tax Payable	Undeposited Funds		0.00
Sales Receipt	03/17/2015	47	Dean, Jim	Undeposited Funds	-SPLIT-	35.00	
Sales Receipt	03/17/2015	47	Dean, Jim	Gym Revenues	Undeposited Funds		35.00
Sales Receipt	03/17/2015	47	Dean, Jim	Sales Tax Payable	Undeposited Funds		0.00
Sales Receipt	03/18/2015	48	Sawyer, Jim	Undeposited Funds	-SPLIT-	60.00	
Sales Receipt	03/18/2015	48	Sawyer, Jim	Registration Fees	Undeposited Funds		25.00
Sales Receipt	03/18/2015	48	Sawyer, Jim	Gym Revenues	Undeposited Funds		35.00
Sales Receipt	03/18/2015	48	Sawyer, Jim	Sales Tax Payable	Undeposited Funds		0.00
Sales Receipt	03/19/2015	49	Sheppert, Christian	Undeposited Funds	-SPLIT-	90.00	
Sales Receipt	03/19/2015	49	Sheppert, Christian	Gym Revenues	Undeposited Funds		90.00

Type	Date	Num	Name	Account	Split	Amount	
Sales Receipt	03/19/2015	49	Sheppert, Christian	Sales Tax Payable	Undeposited Funds	0.00	
Sales Receipt	03/20/2015	50	Austino, Kate	Undeposited Funds	-SPLIT-	35.00	
Sales Receipt	03/20/2015	50	Austino, Kate	Gym Revenues	Undeposited Funds		35.00
Sales Receipt	03/20/2015	50	Austino, Kate	Sales Tax Payable	Undeposited Funds	0.00	
Payment	03/20/2015		Kline, Jerry	Undeposited Funds	Accounts Receivable	35.00	
Payment	03/20/2015		Kline, Jerry	Accounts Receivable	Undeposited Funds		35.00
Payment	03/20/2015		Barnes, Tim	Undeposited Funds	Accounts Receivable	35.00	
Payment	03/20/2015		Barnes, Tim	Accounts Receivable	Undeposited Funds		35.00
Sales Receipt	03/21/2015	51	Russell, Danielle	Undeposited Funds	-SPLIT-	60.00	
Sales Receipt	03/21/2015	51	Russell, Danielle	Registration Fees	Undeposited Funds		25.00
Sales Receipt	03/21/2015	51	Russell, Danielle	Gym Revenues	Undeposited Funds		35.00
Sales Receipt	03/21/2015	51	Russell, Danielle	Sales Tax Payable	Undeposited Funds	0.00	
Sales Receipt	03/21/2015	52	Weekly Sales	Undeposited Funds	-SPLIT-	54.27	
Sales Receipt	03/21/2015	52	Weekly Sales	Merchandise Sales	Undeposited Funds		7.50
Sales Receipt	03/21/2015	52	Weekly Sales	Inventory Asset	Undeposited Funds		0.85
Sales Receipt	03/21/2015	52	Weekly Sales	Cost of Goods Sold	Undeposited Funds	0.85	
Sales Receipt	03/21/2015	52	Weekly Sales	Merchandise Sales	Undeposited Funds		4.00
Sales Receipt	03/21/2015	52	Weekly Sales	Inventory Asset	Undeposited Funds		0.74
Sales Receipt	03/21/2015	52	Weekly Sales	Cost of Goods Sold	Undeposited Funds	0.74	
Sales Receipt	03/21/2015	52	Weekly Sales	Merchandise Sales	Undeposited Funds		6.00
Sales Receipt	03/21/2015	52	Weekly Sales	Inventory Asset	Undeposited Funds		1.11
Sales Receipt	03/21/2015	52	Weekly Sales	Cost of Goods Sold	Undeposited Funds	1.11	
Sales Receipt	03/21/2015	52	Weekly Sales	Merchandise Sales	Undeposited Funds		2.00
Sales Receipt	03/21/2015	52	Weekly Sales	Inventory Asset	Undeposited Funds		0.37
Sales Receipt	03/21/2015	52	Weekly Sales	Cost of Goods Sold	Undeposited Funds	0.37	
Sales Receipt	03/21/2015	52	Weekly Sales	Merchandise Sales	Undeposited Funds		11.25
Sales Receipt	03/21/2015	52	Weekly Sales	Inventory Asset	Undeposited Funds		3.15
Sales Receipt	03/21/2015	52	Weekly Sales	Cost of Goods Sold	Undeposited Funds	3.15	
Sales Receipt	03/21/2015	52	Weekly Sales	Merchandise Sales	Undeposited Funds		9.75
Sales Receipt	03/21/2015	52	Weekly Sales	Inventory Asset	Undeposited Funds		1.35
Sales Receipt	03/21/2015	52	Weekly Sales	Cost of Goods Sold	Undeposited Funds	1.35	
Sales Receipt	03/21/2015	52	Weekly Sales	Merchandise Sales	Undeposited Funds		3.25
Sales Receipt	03/21/2015	52	Weekly Sales	Inventory Asset	Undeposited Funds		0.45
Sales Receipt	03/21/2015	52	Weekly Sales	Cost of Goods Sold	Undeposited Funds	0.45	
Sales Receipt	03/21/2015	52	Weekly Sales	Merchandise Sales	Undeposited Funds		6.50
Sales Receipt	03/21/2015	52	Weekly Sales	Inventory Asset	Undeposited Funds		0.90
Sales Receipt	03/21/2015	52	Weekly Sales	Cost of Goods Sold	Undeposited	0.90	

QUICKBOOKS PRACTICE SET

Type	Date	Num	Name	Account	Split	Amount
Sales Receipt	03/21/2015	52	Iowa Department of Revenue	Sales Tax Payable	Undeposited Funds	4.02
Deposit	03/21/2015			Hometown Bank	-SPLIT-	474.27
Deposit	03/21/2015		Blackburn, Cindy	Undeposited Funds	Hometown Bank	35.00
Deposit	03/21/2015		Blackburn, Cindy	Undeposited Funds	Hometown Bank	35.00
Deposit	03/21/2015		Dean, Jim	Undeposited Funds	Hometown Bank	35.00
Deposit	03/21/2015		Sawyer, Jim	Undeposited Funds	Hometown Bank	60.00
Deposit	03/21/2015		Sheppert, Christian	Undeposited Funds	Hometown Bank	90.00
Deposit	03/21/2015		Austino, Kate	Undeposited Funds	Hometown Bank	35.00
Deposit	03/21/2015		Kline, Jerry	Undeposited Funds	Hometown Bank	35.00
Deposit	03/21/2015		Barnes, Tim	Undeposited Funds	Hometown Bank	35.00
Deposit	03/21/2015		Russell, Danielle	Undeposited Funds	Hometown Bank	60.00
Deposit	03/21/2015		Weekly Sales	Undeposited Funds	Hometown Bank	54.27
Sales Receipt	03/24/2015	53	Linus, Benny	Undeposited Funds	-SPLIT-	60.00
Sales Receipt	03/24/2015	53	Linus, Benny	Registration Fees	Undeposited Funds	25.00
Sales Receipt	03/24/2015	53	Linus, Benny	Gym Revenues	Undeposited Funds	35.00
Sales Receipt	03/24/2015	53	Linus, Benny	Sales Tax Payable	Undeposited Funds	0.00
Credit Memo	03/25/2015	12	Linus, Benny	Accounts Receivable	-SPLIT-	35.00
Credit Memo	03/25/2015	12	Linus, Benny	Gym Revenues	Accounts Receivable	35.00
Credit Memo	03/25/2015	12	Linus, Benny	Sales Tax Payable	Accounts Receivable	0.00
Check	03/25/2015	1028	Linus, Benny	Hometown Bank	Accounts Receivable	35.00
Check	03/25/2015	1028	Linus, Benny	Accounts Receivable	Hometown Bank	35.00
Invoice	03/26/2015	13	Gonzalez, Adrian	Accounts Receivable	-SPLIT-	35.00
Invoice	03/26/2015	13	Gonzalez, Adrian	Gym Revenues	Accounts Receivable	35.00
Invoice	03/26/2015	13	Gonzalez, Adrian	Sales Tax Payable	Accounts Receivable	0.00
Invoice	03/26/2015	14	Steele, Lucy	Accounts Receivable	-SPLIT-	35.00
Invoice	03/26/2015	14	Steele, Lucy	Gym Revenues	Accounts Receivable	35.00
Invoice	03/26/2015	14	Steele, Lucy	Sales Tax Payable	Accounts Receivable	0.00
Invoice	03/26/2015	15	Barnes, Tim	Accounts Receivable	-SPLIT-	35.00
Invoice	03/26/2015	15	Barnes, Tim	Gym Revenues	Accounts Receivable	35.00
Invoice	03/26/2015	15	Barnes, Tim	Sales Tax Payable	Accounts Receivable	0.00
Invoice	03/26/2015	16	Markum, Robert	Accounts Receivable	-SPLIT-	35.00
Invoice	03/26/2015	16	Markum, Robert	Gym Revenues	Accounts Receivable	35.00
Invoice	03/26/2015	16	Markum, Robert	Sales Tax Payable	Accounts Receivable	0.00
Invoice	03/26/2015	17	Layton, Katie	Accounts Receivable	-SPLIT-	35.00
Invoice	03/26/2015	17	Layton, Katie	Gym Revenues	Accounts Receivable	35.00
Invoice	03/26/2015	17	Layton, Katie	Sales Tax Payable	Accounts Receivable	0.00
Invoice	03/26/2015	18	Lockhart, John	Accounts Receivable	-SPLIT-	35.00
Invoice	03/26/2015	18	Lockhart, John	Gym Revenues	Accounts Receivable	35.00

Type	Date	Num	Name	Account	Split	Amount
Invoice	03/26/2015	18	Lockhart, John	Sales Tax Payable	Accounts Receivable	0.00
Invoice	03/26/2015	19	Austino, Kate	Accounts Receivable	-SPLIT-	35.00
Invoice	03/26/2015	19	Austino, Kate	Gym Revenues	Accounts Receivable	35.00
Invoice	03/26/2015	19	Austino, Kate	Sales Tax Payable	Accounts Receivable	0.00
Invoice	03/26/2015	20	Sawyer, Jim	Accounts Receivable	-SPLIT-	35.00
Invoice	03/26/2015	20	Sawyer, Jim	Gym Revenues	Accounts Receivable	35.00
Invoice	03/26/2015	20	Sawyer, Jim	Sales Tax Payable	Accounts Receivable	0.00
Check	03/27/2015	1029	Rob's Repairs	Hometown Bank	Repairs and Maintenance	220.00
Check	03/27/2015	1029	Rob's Repairs	Repairs and Maintenance	Hometown Bank	220.00
Sales Receipt	03/28/2015	54	Gonzalez, Adrian	Undeposited Funds	-SPLIT-	70.00
Sales Receipt	03/28/2015	54	Gonzalez, Adrian	Gym Revenues	Undeposited Funds	70.00
Sales Receipt	03/28/2015	54	Gonzalez, Adrian	Sales Tax Payable	Undeposited Funds	0.00
Bill Pmt - Check	03/30/2015	1030	City of Springfield	Hometown Bank	Accounts Payable	86.45
Bill Pmt - Check	03/30/2015	1030	City of Springfield	Accounts Payable	Hometown Bank	86.45
Bill Pmt - Check	03/30/2015	1031	Fit Foods, Inc.	Hometown Bank	Accounts Payable	84.24
Bill Pmt - Check	03/30/2015	1031	Fit Foods, Inc.	Accounts Payable	Hometown Bank	84.24
Bill Pmt - Check	03/30/2015	1032	Metro Electric	Hometown Bank	Accounts Payable	178.86
Bill Pmt - Check	03/30/2015	1032	Metro Electric	Accounts Payable	Hometown Bank	178.86
Bill Pmt - Check	03/30/2015	1033	Time Warner	Hometown Bank	Accounts Payable	147.62
Bill Pmt - Check	03/30/2015	1033	Time Warner	Accounts Payable	Hometown Bank	147.62
Bill Pmt - Check	03/30/2015	1034	Waste Management	Hometown Bank	Accounts Payable	45.00
Bill Pmt - Check	03/30/2015	1034	Waste Management	Accounts Payable	Hometown Bank	45.00
Bill	03/31/2015		Time Warner	Accounts Payable	Phone / Internet	147.62
Bill	03/31/2015		Time Warner	Phone / Internet	Accounts Payable	147.62
Bill	03/31/2015		Metro Electric	Accounts Payable	Electricity	128.86
Bill	03/31/2015		Metro Electric	Electricity	Accounts Payable	128.86
Bill	03/31/2015		City of Springfield	Accounts Payable	Water	79.45
Bill	03/31/2015		City of Springfield	Water	Accounts Payable	79.45
Bill	03/31/2015		Waste Management	Accounts Payable	Trash Removal	45.00
Bill	03/31/2015		Waste Management	Trash Removal	Accounts Payable	45.00
Sales Receipt	03/31/2015	55	Weekly Sales	Undeposited Funds	-SPLIT-	96.39
Sales Receipt	03/31/2015	55	Weekly Sales	Merchandise Sales	Undeposited Funds	15.00
Sales Receipt	03/31/2015	55	Weekly Sales	Inventory Asset	Undeposited Funds	1.70
Sales Receipt	03/31/2015	55	Weekly Sales	Cost of Goods Sold	Undeposited Funds	1.70
Sales Receipt	03/31/2015	55	Weekly Sales	Merchandise Sales	Undeposited Funds	6.00
Sales Receipt	03/31/2015	55	Weekly Sales	Inventory Asset	Undeposited Funds	1.11
Sales Receipt	03/31/2015	55	Weekly Sales	Cost of Goods Sold	Undeposited Funds	1.11
Sales Receipt	03/31/2015	55	Weekly Sales	Merchandise Sales	Undeposited Funds	6.00

QUICKBOOKS PRACTICE SET

Type	Date	Num	Name	Account	Split	Debit	Credit
Sales Receipt	03/31/2015	55	Weekly Sales	Inventory Asset	Undeposited Funds		1.11
Sales Receipt	03/31/2015	55	Weekly Sales	Cost of Goods Sold	Undeposited Funds	1.11	
Sales Receipt	03/31/2015	55	Weekly Sales	Merchandise Sales	Undeposited Funds		10.00
Sales Receipt	03/31/2015	55	Weekly Sales	Inventory Asset	Undeposited Funds		1.85
Sales Receipt	03/31/2015	55	Weekly Sales	Cost of Goods Sold	Undeposited Funds	1.85	
Sales Receipt	03/31/2015	55	Weekly Sales	Merchandise Sales	Undeposited Funds		18.75
Sales Receipt	03/31/2015	55	Weekly Sales	Inventory Asset	Undeposited Funds		5.25
Sales Receipt	03/31/2015	55	Weekly Sales	Cost of Goods Sold	Undeposited Funds	5.25	
Sales Receipt	03/31/2015	55	Weekly Sales	Merchandise Sales	Undeposited Funds		7.50
Sales Receipt	03/31/2015	55	Weekly Sales	Inventory Asset	Undeposited Funds		2.10
Sales Receipt	03/31/2015	55	Weekly Sales	Cost of Goods Sold	Undeposited Funds	2.10	
Sales Receipt	03/31/2015	55	Weekly Sales	Merchandise Sales	Undeposited Funds		6.50
Sales Receipt	03/31/2015	55	Weekly Sales	Inventory Asset	Undeposited Funds		0.90
Sales Receipt	03/31/2015	55	Weekly Sales	Cost of Goods Sold	Undeposited Funds	0.90	
Sales Receipt	03/31/2015	55	Weekly Sales	Merchandise Sales	Undeposited Funds		6.50
Sales Receipt	03/31/2015	55	Weekly Sales	Inventory Asset	Undeposited Funds		0.90
Sales Receipt	03/31/2015	55	Weekly Sales	Cost of Goods Sold	Undeposited Funds	0.90	
Sales Receipt	03/31/2015	55	Weekly Sales	Merchandise Sales	Undeposited Funds		13.00
Sales Receipt	03/31/2015	55	Weekly Sales	Inventory Asset	Undeposited Funds		1.80
Sales Receipt	03/31/2015	55	Weekly Sales	Cost of Goods Sold	Undeposited Funds	1.80	
Sales Receipt	03/31/2015	55	Iowa Department of Revenue	Sales Tax Payable	Undeposited Funds		7.14
Deposit	03/31/2015			Hometown Bank	-SPLIT-	226.39	
Deposit	03/31/2015		Linus, Benny	Undeposited Funds	Hometown Bank		60.00
Deposit	03/31/2015		Gonzalez, Adrian	Undeposited Funds	Hometown Bank		70.00
Deposit	03/31/2015		Weekly Sales	Undeposited Funds	Hometown Bank		96.39

Made in the USA
Las Vegas, NV
31 January 2022

42729680R00061